THE BEDFORD SERIES IN HISTORY AND CULTURE

The Oil Crisis
of 1973–1974

A Brief History with Documents

Related Titles in
THE BEDFORD SERIES IN HISTORY AND CULTURE
Advisory Editors: Lynn Hunt, *University of California, Los Angeles*
David W. Blight, *Yale University*
Bonnie G. Smith, *Rutgers University*
Natalie Zemon Davis, *Princeton University*
Ernest R. May, *Harvard University*

THE BEDFORD SERIES IN HISTORY AND CULTURE

The Oil Crisis of 1973–1974

A Brief History with Documents

Karen R. Merrill

Williams College

BEDFORD/ST. MARTIN'S   Boston   ♦   New York

For Theo and Dash

For Bedford/St. Martin's

Publisher for History: Mary V. Dougherty
Director of Development for History: Jane Knetzger
Developmental Editor: Ann Kirby-Payne
Editorial Assistant: Laurel Damashek
Senior Production Supervisor: Joe Ford
Production Associate: Maureen O'Neill
Executive Marketing Manager: Jenna Bookin Barry
Project Management: Books By Design, Inc.
Text Design: Claire Seng-Niemoeller
Indexing: Books By Design, Inc.
Cover Design: Billy Boardman
Cover Art: *Gas Shortage Sign in Connecticut, 1974.* © Owen Franken/CORBIS
Composition: Stratford Publishing Services, Inc.
Printing and Binding: RR Donnelley & Sons Company

President: Joan E. Feinberg
Editorial Director: Denise B. Wydra
Director of Marketing: Karen Melton Soeltz
Director of Editing, Design, and Production: Marcia Cohen
Manager, Publishing Services: Emily Berleth

Library of Congress Control Number: 2006935058

For information, write: Bedford/St. Martin's, 75 Arlington Street, Boston, MA 02116
(617-399-4000)

ISBN-10: 0-312-40922-2
ISBN-13: 978-0-312-40922-7

Acknowledgments

Acknowledgments and copyrights are continued at the back of the book on page 166, which constitutes an extension of the copyright page.

Foreword

The Bedford Series in History and Culture is designed so that readers can study the past as historians do.

The historian's first task is finding the evidence. Documents, letters, memoirs, interviews, pictures, movies, novels, or poems can provide facts and clues. Then the historian questions and compares the sources. There is more to do than in a courtroom, for hearsay evidence is welcome, and the historian is usually looking for answers beyond act and motive. Different views of an event may be as important as a single verdict. How a story is told may yield as much information as what it says.

Along the way the historian seeks help from other historians and perhaps from specialists in other disciplines. Finally, it is time to write, to decide on an interpretation and how to arrange the evidence for readers.

Each book in this series contains an important historical document or group of documents, each document a witness from the past and open to interpretation in different ways. The documents are combined with some element of historical narrative—an introduction or a biographical essay, for example—that provides students with an analysis of the primary source material and important background information about the world in which it was produced.

Each book in the series focuses on a specific topic within a specific historical period. Each provides a basis for lively thought and discussion about several aspects of the topic and the historian's role. Each is short enough (and inexpensive enough) to be a reasonable one-week assignment in a college course. Whether as classroom or personal reading, each book in the series provides firsthand experience of the challenge—and fun—of discovering, recreating, and interpreting the past.

Lynn Hunt
David W. Blight
Bonnie G. Smith
Natalie Zemon Davis
Ernest R. May

Preface

The oil crisis of 1973–1974 constituted a watershed event in American history. Following decades of U.S. economic growth that depended on cheap oil, the crisis signaled a new era of diminished expectations for many Americans as well as a seemingly radical transformation in international politics. Despite warning signs throughout 1972 and 1973 that the geopolitics of oil were rapidly changing, Americans were stunned to find out on October 19, 1973, that the Arab members of the Organization of Petroleum Exporting Countries (OPEC) would use the "oil weapon." Those countries instituted an embargo on all shipments of oil to the United States, hoping to elicit changes in U.S. and European foreign policy toward the Middle East. Throughout that fall and early winter, OPEC as a whole also doubled, then tripled, and ultimately quadrupled the per-barrel price of oil, quickly fueling inflationary forces within the American economy that would reverberate into the early 1980s. Gas lines formed at service stations, and panic buying ensued. In New England, where most people heated their homes with oil, conversations revolved around one topic: how to absorb the price of heat into the family budget. President Richard Nixon implored citizens to turn down their thermostats and carpool, while Congress passed legislation to reduce the speed limit on U.S. highways so that vehicles would burn gasoline more efficiently. Congress also extended daylight savings time through the winter in order to increase the number of daylight hours in hopes that it would reduce electricity and heating demands in the late afternoon.

In January 1974, as officials in Washington prepared the American public for possible gasoline rationing, it appeared that the "American Century," marked by rapid economic growth and rising global power, was already at a close. Although the embargo lasted only until March 1974, oil prices remained high throughout the 1970s, and most Americans experienced the decade as one of economic limits rather than opportunity.

This volume is the first of its kind to help students understand the historical significance and long-term ramifications of the oil crisis of 1973–1974. It argues that the events of this time served, on the one hand, to illuminate a set of tensions about the place of oil in American life, tensions that had been growing in importance throughout the twentieth century and, on the other hand, to presage the conflicts about oil production and consumption that would mark the global politics of the late twentieth and early twenty-first centuries. Given that the question of America's access to the world's petroleum reserves will only become more pressing in the years to follow, learning about Americans' past relationship to this resource should be an essential part of students' encounters with American history.

The introduction to the volume tells the story of the oil industry in the United States and abroad from the mid-nineteenth century to the twenty-first century. Oil was involved in many of the most significant transformations of the twentieth century—from the waging of war to the creation of suburbia; from the growing international importance of the Middle East to Americans' changing notions of the natural world. More broadly, the introduction emphasizes the themes that students will find woven throughout the documents:

- the centrality of oil to the global economy
- the geopolitical battles over securing America's oil needs
- the anxiety about the nation's post–World War II consumer habits
- the environmental concerns about America's oil use

The historical documents follow in five sections that explore different observers' interpretations of the crisis and how it shaped the economic, political, and cultural life of America. Chapter 1 examines U.S.– Middle East relations prior to the oil crisis. It includes telegrams and memoranda documenting government and industry reactions to the formation of OPEC in 1960, and the changing political and business climate in the years that followed. The embargo itself is the focus of Chapter 2, which documents reactions to the crisis from the government, the oil industry, and everyday citizens. Selections here range from contemporary political cartoons to President Nixon's speech on the energy emergency. In Chapter 3, the documents focus on the relationship between consumer culture, the environment, and the changing geopolitics of oil in the early 1970s. Chapter 4 examines the wide range of opinions about political options that emerged in the immediate aftermath of the crisis. Documents include the contrasting visions of oil policy presented by Presidents Jimmy Carter and Ronald Reagan. The final chapter explores the legacies of the crisis, inviting readers to consider how the lessons of the 1970s have (or have not) affected American culture and environmental and foreign policy in the decades that followed.

Each chapter and document is introduced with a thoughtful headnote that provides an overview of the contexts and connections of the primary source material. A chronology at the end of the book lays out the history of America's reliance on petroleum. Additional resources include a 1972 contemporary map of oil fields in the Middle East, questions for consideration, and a bibliographic essay guiding students to further reading.

ACKNOWLEDGMENTS

This book is the product of much collaboration. I owe many thanks to my students at Williams College, especially those who have taken my History of Oil seminar and whose insights have deepened my understanding of the subject. Funding from Williams College also moved this book along, and it allowed me to work with five talented student research assistants: Oliver Sloman, Erik Wobus, Ben Cronin, Ananda Burra, and Marissa Doran. My thanks to Marissa for her comments on the manuscript. I was fortunate also to have the help of Sandy Zepka, who keeps the Center for Environmental Studies running smoothly. Her organizational skills in tracking copyright permissions allowed me to focus on other aspects of preparing the manuscript. Finally, the library staffs at both Amherst College and Williams College, especially Walter Komorowski, were uniformly helpful in the process of collecting documents for this book.

I am very grateful to the following people at Bedford/St. Martin's Press for encouraging this project: David Blight, Patricia Rossi, Mary Dougherty, and Jane Knetzger. Daniel Horowitz at Smith College gave me superb advice about how to construct this volume in its early stages. Ann Kirby-Payne, more than anyone else, helped me to see the project through to completion. She brought to her job as editor immense patience, optimism, good judgment, and clarity, and she coached me through several tight deadlines with great grace. Emily Berleth and Laurel Damashek at Bedford/St. Martin's and Nancy Benjamin at Books By Design ably guided the book in its final phases.

As always, my family far and near lent their support and enthusiasm.

In particular, thanks to Martha Umphrey for showing me true generosity in thought and deed. Although, as a historian, I am always looking to the past, my sons Theo and Dash help me to keep an eye on the future. They also keep me laughing, for which I'm very grateful. I dedicate this book to them because I know that they and their generation will have the intelligence, heart, and courage to solve the energy challenges that lie ahead.

Karen R. Merrill

Contents

APPENDIXES

Illustrations

PART ONE

Introduction:
A Brief History of Oil

In mid-December 1973, tens of thousands of drivers on highways across America found themselves ensnarled in colossal traffic jams that stretched for miles and lasted for hours. Drivers fumed, stomping out of their cars in frustration and peering into the distance to determine the cause of the massive backups. But these were no ordinary traffic jams. In states such as Arkansas, Connecticut, New York, Ohio, and Florida, independent truckers had parked their rigs on freeways, turnpikes, and toll roads to protest the high price of gasoline. The most prolonged incident occurred on the Ohio Turnpike, where the protest "strangled traffic between Cleveland and Toledo for nearly 24 hours."[1]

Struggling to absorb the price increases, independent truckers had stopped traffic to protest not only the price of gas but also what they saw as the ineffectiveness of government efforts to control the price. In September 1973, it cost a trucker about 27 cents a gallon to fill up the tank. By December, that figure had jumped to between 45 and 51 cents a gallon, and many truckers accused service stations of price gouging. Motorists stuck in the traffic jams might have been frustrated by the truckers' form of protest, but they certainly sympathized with the target. The high price of gasoline left few Americans untouched.

The spike in gas prices had not come out of nowhere, of course. It had come in response to the most serious disruption of the world's oil supply since World War II, during which the U.S. government had rationed gasoline at home in order to fuel the war effort abroad. This time, the oil shortage and price increase had resulted from a decision made by oil-producing countries in the Middle East to embargo their oil in protest of U.S. foreign policy toward the Middle East. In response to America's support of Israel after Egypt and Syria's attack on that country in early October 1973, the Arab members of the Organization of Petroleum Exporting Countries (OPEC) decided to use their countries' oil resources as a political weapon, choosing first to cut back dramatically on the amount of oil shipped to the United States and then to prohibit all oil shipments to America.[2] OPEC as a whole sharply increased the price its members received for each barrel of oil. This move ratcheted up fuel costs for American consumers, who were already grappling with rising consumer prices and a devalued dollar. By using oil as a weapon, OPEC sent a stinging message that reverberated throughout the U.S. economy.

These events alone would have shocked the country, hitting ordinary Americans hard in their wallets and making them feel helpless in the face of countries that had previously wielded very little power internationally. The timing of the crisis was also crucial, for it occurred in the midst of a nationwide debate about the state of the environment and the future of American consumption in a climate of increasing inflation. In both of these realms, oil was already part of the equation. Since the late 1960s, Americans had grown increasingly concerned about the environmental risks posed by their reliance on oil, in terms of oil spills at sea, the risks associated with the production and use of petrochemicals, and air quality. By 1973, Congress had passed several environmental laws, but the oil crisis nonetheless served as evidence for environmentalists that the United States needed to dramatically change course and enact policies that would encourage, even force, Americans to conserve oil and explore other sources of energy.

The oil crisis also provoked wide-ranging conversation about the postwar consumer economy in the United States. The period from 1945 to the early 1970s saw the country achieve its most dramatic economic growth in its history, marked by high profits, increased productivity, and low unemployment. This economy had been built on the expanding production of consumer goods—items such as televisions, washing machines, blenders, and automobiles—and had allowed a broadening middle class greater access to more consumer goods. Both the government and ordinary citizens were well aware that

America's economic engine was fueled by its appetite for consumer goods and that appetite would continue to grow.

But confidence in the economy began to falter as the postwar boom showed signs of weakening in the late 1960s and early 1970s. Economic competition from other countries, predominantly West Germany and Japan, began cutting into the market for America's exported goods, causing U.S. manufacturing profits to plummet 29.5 percent in comparison to the previous two decades.[3] Workers quickly felt the consequences of rapidly falling profits, as real wage growth effectively came to a halt in 1973. (It would barely inch upward for many years thereafter.) Thus, when OPEC announced its oil embargo and price increases in the fall of 1973, ordinary Americans were already facing much more limited economic options than they had ten years before. The steep spike in oil prices only made their economic future seem that much more precarious.

Oil touched virtually every part of the American economy. In addition to the multitude of consumer goods made out of oil—particularly plastics—gasoline powered all forms of transportation, and transportation brought consumer goods to markets. The oil crisis forced experts and citizens alike to wonder when and how consumer capitalism would rebound to its earlier heights if scarce supplies of oil (or simply very expensive oil) continued to drive up prices across the economy.

In addition to provoking deep anxiety about the domestic economy and the environment, the emergence of OPEC as an international political player also made Americans very nervous. Even after the Arab members of OPEC ended the embargo in March 1974—following weeks of negotiations with the United States and with the hope that tensions between Israel and its neighbors were easing—OPEC maintained an "imperium" over oil prices that put it at the center of world politics throughout the 1970s.[4] For many people in the United States and abroad, OPEC's effective use of the "oil weapon" weakened the nation's standing internationally. Along with the formal end to American participation in the Vietnam War and the emerging Watergate scandal in Richard Nixon's presidency, the oil crisis suggested to many that America's postwar power was waning. Though not the last oil crisis faced by this country, it was the first and only one to force Americans at all levels to question so deeply the very material basis of U.S. economic might and America's political position in the world.

This book opens the door to that questioning and explores the variety of ways in which Americans responded to the oil crisis. Whereas environmentalists charged that Americans needed to take a crash course in conservation, others argued that such thinking played on people's fears and that human ingenuity would provide options for reducing Americans' dependence on petroleum. Amid widespread criticism of Arab political leaders, many commentators roundly condemned both American political officials and American oil companies in the Persian Gulf region that acquiesced to OPEC's demands and made profits on the high price of oil. Given the great complexities of the industry and the global market for oil, there was no end to the blame game during or after the crisis.

To explain the significance of the oil crisis of 1973–1974, this introduction provides a historical context, beginning with the early organization of the oil business in the mid- to late nineteenth century. This context, which is left out of most narratives of modern America, will illuminate why the oil crisis stands as such a signal event in the twentieth century, especially in the decades following World War II. After nearly thirty years in which the United States had risen to the level of a global superpower, the crisis called into question the very foundations of America's international status and national identity. It showed that a group of politically weak countries could nonetheless exercise tremendous economic power over the United States. It indicated that, despite the fact that the nation was one of the two most powerful countries in the world (the Soviet Union being the other), the United States increasingly depended on oil that originated beyond its shores. And finally, the crisis threatened the first principle of America's astounding postwar economic growth: access to cheap oil and gasoline. In other words, the oil crisis cut to the core of American assumptions.

Its legacy, however, may be more difficult to ascertain, as American leaders and ordinary citizens took away diverse lessons from the events. For some, the powerlessness that the United States seemed to exhibit during the embargo indicated that the nation needed to assert its presence more aggressively in world politics, even if that meant potential military engagements. As it turned out, by the end of the decade, a Democratic president, Jimmy Carter, would formally declare that the United States would protect its national interests in Persian Gulf oil through military means if necessary. Other Americans believed that the oil crisis fundamentally revolved around the country's outsize consumption of natural resources, particularly oil. For them, the lessons required Americans to transform their attitudes about the way they lived—how far they drove their cars, the appliances they used, and the things they bought. Many Americans likely held a constellation of views that did not fall easily into either of these two categories and that came down to a deep belief that such a crisis should not happen again.

But oil crises did occur after 1973. Although they had different causes than the first oil shock, each one has reminded Americans of the country's increasing dependence on foreign oil. In 1973, for instance, the United States imported about 33 percent of its oil. In 2005, that number stood near 60 percent. As that percentage inevitably increases in the years to come—especially the proportion imported from Saudi Arabia—Americans will likely revisit the questions of the early 1970s, but in a world with a vastly more complex economic network. And as worldwide supplies of oil begin to dwindle in the coming decades, people around the globe will face the challenge of developing ways out of the petroleum age.

THE UNITED STATES AS OIL PRODUCER

Oil became big business in the immediate wake of the first oil discovery at Titusville, Pennsylvania, in 1859. Soon after, enterprising men built refineries to take advantage of the emerging market in kerosene, a fuel refined from oil and used for illumination. One of those men was John D. Rockefeller, a young businessman from Cleveland, whose name would soon become synonymous with *monopoly.* In the decades following the Civil War, Rockefeller built what had begun as a small refinery business into the Standard Oil Company. Rockefeller's power and control over the American oil industry would grow throughout the late nineteenth century to include not only oil production but also the refining and marketing of kerosene. He also made profitable deals with the railroads that transported his products. Rockefeller's devotion to the strategy of "vertical integration"—that is, the practice of controlling all phases of the oil production process, from getting the oil out of the ground to refining it to transporting it to selling it to consumers—allowed him to establish a solid monopoly of the kerosene market. According to some estimates, Standard Oil controlled about 85 percent of the market in 1890.

Rockefeller did not confine his empire to American shores, and as early as the 1880s, he was shipping oil to European and Asian markets. He produced, in addition to kerosene, the first truly major multinational oil company in America. But his monopolizing of the kerosene market did not escape the attention of the federal government. In

1911, the Supreme Court upheld a lower court decision that Standard Oil was in violation of the Sherman Antitrust Act of 1890, then ordered the company to dissolve within six months. What emerged were several Standard Oil companies operating in different states.

Although the government broke up Standard Oil, Americans would remain suspicious of the oil industry throughout the twentieth century. For instance, during the oil crisis of 1973–1974, critics often charged that the American oil companies operating in the Persian Gulf had joined together to exert monopolistic control over the oil market. Indeed, the largest company producing oil in the Middle East had been created from the smaller Standard Oil companies resulting from the 1911 ruling.

The oil industry also took off in Texas in the early twentieth century. The first oil strike there occurred in 1901, near Beaumont, on the Gulf Coast. As in Titusville, the discovery set off a series of oil booms across the state—and later in Oklahoma as well—that would continue for decades.

In 1930, a determined independent by the name of Columbus Marion "Dad" Joiner drilled the first well in East Texas, a region that would ultimately produce about 4.5 billion barrels of oil. At first the strike appeared to be a godsend to the state, which was suffering through the depths of the Great Depression. But even with oil, there can sometimes be too much of a good thing. In part because of the desperate financial times, the East Texas oil boom drew scores of men and women, known as "independents" or "wildcatters," into the oil business. The result was tremendous overproduction, which sent the price of oil spiraling downward until it reached only ten cents a barrel—about the cost of a loaf of bread or a dozen eggs. Though extremely wary of any kind of government regulation of their industry, independents nonetheless agreed to allow two regulatory bodies to oversee oil production.

The first was the Texas Railroad Commission (TRC). Originally formed in 1891 to curb monopolistic practices among railroad owners, the TRC was now empowered to establish quotas on the amount of oil that could be pumped from Texas wells. By curbing the supply side of oil, the TRC hoped to raise prices so that Texas oil producers could make money on their investments. Although some oil producers in the region tried to skirt the regulations by exceeding the quotas and selling oil on the black market, the TRC largely succeeded in achieving its goal. The second regulatory body, the Interstate Oil Compact Commission (IOCC), was formed in 1935 to allow a handful of petroleum-producing states to cooperate in curbing overproduction and waste in order to maintain profitable prices.

By the 1930s, the American oil industry had developed into a complex constellation of firms and people. Some companies consisted of only one or two employees; others, such as the largest Standard Oil firms—including Standard Oil of New Jersey and Standard Oil of California (Socal)—would soon emerge as global players.

THE GLOBAL SEARCH FOR OIL

The complexity of the U.S. oil industry was a source of great pride for many American oilmen, for it stood in sharp contrast to oil operations in other countries. By the 1930s, the global search for oil revolved around a handful of large companies because, for the most part, small, independent companies or individuals simply did not have the capital or business and political connections necessary to build oil operations outside the United States.

Not surprisingly, the oil companies that were most active internationally were based in European countries that had established colonies throughout the world. Consider, for example, Royal Dutch/Shell. The product of a 1907 merger between two oil companies—Shell of England and Royal Dutch of the Netherlands—it dominated the East Asian market, where both countries had either a colonial presence or sought to exercise a powerful influence. Like Rockefeller's Standard Oil, Royal Dutch/Shell grew into a large, vertically integrated company, operating at all levels of the industry, from exploration to drilling to refining to marketing. Over the decades, it extended its reach to other parts of the world. Today it is the dominant company in Nigeria, for instance—among the most productive oil-exporting countries in the world—despite a great deal of protest and violence directed against the company's industrial practices.

At about the same time that the merger occurred between Royal Dutch and Shell, a much smaller British firm appeared on the scene that would eventually play an even greater political role. In 1901—the same year that Texas became an oil-producing state—an Englishman named William Knox D'Arcy gained the right to drill for oil for sixty years in Persia (now Iran), in return for providing that country with royalty payments. D'Arcy's deal, known as an oil concession, would give the British a remarkable leg up in their competition with the Russians to exercise influence over Iran—a competition that extended back into the previous century. Initially, however, his attempts to find oil seemed fruitless. In addition to not finding any oil, his Anglo-Persian Oil Company (later the Anglo-Iranian Oil Company) had almost no business infrastructure, and raising money for continued exploration was extremely difficult, since many potential investors found it a risky proposition. D'Arcy finally cobbled together enough money to make possible a successful strike in the southwestern Iranian oil fields of Masjed Soleyman in 1908. But that was just the beginning of his logistical and financial problems, as Anglo-Persian had to figure out how to get the oil to a refinery (it would end up building one in Abadan) and then how to get the product to market (it worked with a Royal Dutch/Shell subsidiary).

The oil field proved to be huge, and in one of the most significant events in the history of oil, the British government decided in 1914 to buy 51 percent of Anglo-Persian. The British government had a good reason to want to be directly involved in the industry: It had shifted the fuel source for its military from coal to oil some years earlier. After World War I and the establishment of British protectorates in the Middle East, Britain exercised more power over Persia (renamed Iran in 1935). One well-respected journalist in the 1920s even predicted that Britain's stranglehold over Middle Eastern oil supplies and America's commercial expansionism would lead to inevitable conflict between the two countries and spark the next "Great War."[5]

That did not happen, of course, but many American oilmen viewed the British government's direct financial stake in the Iranian oil industry with alarm. In fact, the British were everywhere during the first decades of twentieth-century oil exploration: the Middle East, Asia, and even—much to the chagrin of many Americans—the Western Hemisphere, where huge quantities of oil were found in Mexico and Venezuela in the 1910s and 1920s.

Of these, Mexico would prove the most politically important because in 1938, it nationalized its oil industry. This meant that the Mexican government took over the ownership and running of all oil operations, which had previously been under the ownership and control of a variety of largely British and American companies. For many years, political leaders and others in Mexico had harshly criticized foreign oil companies for their ruthless exploitation of both the country's oil resources and the Mexican workers whom the industry employed. By this point, however, the oil boom in Mexico was waning, and Venezuela's star was on the rise. In the 1930s, Venezuela was thought to have some of the largest oil reserves in the world, and both Standard Oil of New Jersey and Royal Dutch/Shell were well-placed there to take advantage of those reserves.

On the eve of World War II, oilmen around the globe would have observed several things. First, in the leading oil-producing country in the world, the United States, the Texas Railroad Commission and the new Interstate Oil Compact Commission were doing their jobs in trying to regulate supply and demand, and by the mid-1930s prices were stabilizing. The success of the TRC, in fact, served as a model for petroleum exporting countries such as Saudi Arabia, Iran, and Venezuela in the years leading up to the creation of OPEC. Second, the oilmen's experience with Mexico's nationalization made them wary of mixing oil with the politics of the foreign countries in which they operated, especially when it came to addressing labor conflicts, which had been a flashpoint for American and British firms in Mexico. In particular, the British government and the management of the Anglo-Iranian Oil Company feared giving ground on this question, believing that responding positively to labor's demands would entail losing control of their companies. Soon, however, the oilmen's fear of nationalization would make them more open to considering other options, such as giving exporting countries a greater share of the profits. Third, a few American oilmen could be heard voicing their concern that, productive as the East Texas fields were, the amount of oil to be found in the United States was limited and that the industry needed to enter the global search for oil more aggressively.

That search had already begun in the Middle East, and the results were encouraging. By 1938, with a sixty-year concession in hand from the Saudi kingdom, Standard Oil of California (now Chevron) and the Texas Company (now Texaco) had joined to create a new firm in Saudi Arabia, Caltex. That year, Caltex successfully drilled its first oil well. Gulf Oil and Standard Oil of New Jersey had begun exploring other parts of the Persian Gulf region, indicating that the British would soon see serious competition.

OIL, ENEMIES, AND THE POSTWAR WORLD

World War II changed almost every aspect of the oil industry, both in the United States and throughout the world. For one thing, many key battles revolved around gaining access to oil fields and refineries. For instance, the repeated attempts of the Nazi general Erwin Rommel to beat back Allied troops in North Africa came as a result of Germany's

great need for the oil resources of the Middle East. Both the Allies
and the Axis powers used staggering quantities of oil. During one
month of bombing Japanese shipping routes, for example, the United
States used approximately 150 million gallons of aviation fuel. To meet
the military demand for oil—as well as to keep America's domestic
economy running—required the direct intervention of the government, which occurred when Congress authorized the creation of the
Petroleum Administration for War (PAW). Consisting largely of men
with experience in the oil industry, the PAW emphasized the importance of oil conservation, both with American consumers and with oil
producers, as the agency needed every drop of oil it could get for the
war effort. In contrast to the 1930s, those East Texas oil fields could
barely produce enough oil to keep Allied planes, ships, and tanks
moving.

While the PAW worried whether American oil producers could
keep fueling the war, the Roosevelt administration had larger concerns about American oil supplies in the future. Evidence was gathering that the United States could not rely on its domestic oil supply
forever, a fact that had implications not only for the American economy but also for the U.S. military, which wanted a secure supply of oil
in case of future wars. In 1943, Roosevelt sent two petroleum geologists on a secret mission to the Middle East, and they confirmed that
the Persian Gulf nations would be the center of the next big oil boom.
The Roosevelt administration initially responded by proposing various
ways in which the U.S. government could take part in the American
oil industry's search for and production of oil in Saudi Arabia. But
American oilmen shot down these ideas, preferring that the government stay out of their business. Instead, Chevron and Texaco teamed
up with two other companies, Standard Oil of New Jersey (now
Exxon) and Socony-Vacuum (now Mobil), to create Aramco. This new
company would attract the capital it needed to ramp up operations in
Saudi Arabia.

There were still a great many questions about Aramco's oil concession in particular and the American oil industry's emerging presence
in the Middle East in general. The first had to do with the nature of
U.S. commercial power abroad. Most American leaders, and most oilmen, saw Aramco's operations in Saudi Arabia as a good thing for the
Saudis, believing that oil production would bring much-needed economic development to the country. That the U.S. government decided
not to become directly involved financially in Aramco saved it from the
taint of colonialism, something the British could not escape in the

Anglo Iranian Oil Company. Although the British did not exercise actual colonial power in Iran, their heavy-handedness in dealing with the Iranians seemed to many a holdover of old-style imperial politics. Aramco executives were keen to avoid acting like the British, and yet they often turned a blind eye to such critical matters as the working and living conditions of their Saudi employees. Opportunities for job training and advancement were lacking, as Americans filled the ranks of the technical staff. Furthermore, Aramco segregated Saudi workers in separate camps, sparking labor unrest. Thus, although Aramco was not attached to a regime of colonial governance, it operated under a similar logic that made it difficult for Saudis to advance in the industry.

In the context of the postwar world, these problems had profound implications. The end of World War II not only halted Hitler, but it also saw colonial regimes begin to fall around the globe. Anticolonial political movements gained strength in countries that had either experienced colonialism firsthand or felt the powerful influence of European nations, as had been the case throughout the Middle East after World War I. When it came to relations between the oil companies and the exporting countries, the balance of power began to shift even before the end of World War II. For example, in 1943 the Venezuelan government, on the heels of regime change, successfully negotiated the first "fifty-fifty" deal with Standard Oil of New Jersey and Royal Dutch/Shell. According to this deal, the government would receive approximately the same amount in oil royalties and taxes as the companies would earn in profits. In 1950, Saudi Arabia worked out a similar deal with Aramco.

In contrast, the Anglo-Iranian Oil Company (AIOC) refused to increase the Iranian government's share of its oil profits. For many Iranians, this refusal represented something greater than lost revenue. Oil was the country's primary "bankable" resource, and both the wealth it generated and the operational control over it lay in the hands of the British, whose behavior in Iran provoked ire and distrust. By early 1951, the stakes had increased in the growing conflict between the AIOC and the Iranian government, as the leader of the country's opposition movement, Mohammed Mossadegh, called for the nationalization of the oil industry. With the memory of Mexican nationalization still fresh—and given the fact that Britain relied almost entirely on Iranian oil for its fuel needs—Mossadegh's political aim represented a grave threat to the British, who would be forced to give up their long-term investment in Iranian oil development. Mossadegh's belief that the nation's oil belonged to the Iranians galvanized political support, and when he became prime minister in April 1951, nationalization became the law. All British oil properties were expropriated, sparking a legal battle over the terms by which the Iranian government would compensate the AIOC.

But the AIOC did not want compensation; it wanted to restore its oil operations in Iran. And if nationalization revolved around who would control and profit from the Iranian oil fields, much more than material resources was at stake, especially for the United States. Fearful that the Soviet Union would gain influence in Arab oil producing countries such as Iran and Saudi Arabia, the United States saw the region as an ideological and strategic battleground in the early cold war, and the countries in the region found themselves caught up in this global struggle. To the incoming Eisenhower administration in early 1953, Mossadegh represented a threat not only because he had kicked the British out of Iran but also because he appeared to make the region more unstable and vulnerable to Soviet influence. From Eisenhower's cold war perspective, Mossadegh's anticolonial regime could easily fall prey to the Communists. With that fear driving the U.S. government, and with the British wanting to take back their Iranian oil operations, the two wartime allies orchestrated a coup d'état in 1953. Mossadegh was overthrown and sent to prison, and the AIOC returned to Iran.

Such a blatant violation of Iranian sovereignty speaks to the growing significance of oil in international politics in the 1950s, and the lengths to which the United States and its allies would go in the quest to meet their petroleum needs. Mossadegh was not the only leader in the Middle East to provoke cold war anxieties. The U.S. government saw a particular threat in Egypt's Gamal Abdel Nasser, who was involved in a military coup in 1952 and came to power in 1954. Nasser became a popular leader not only in Egypt but also across the region because of his vociferous anti-British views, his nationalist ideals, and his belief that the Arab countries should create a Pan-Arab political bloc. He had no problem confronting the West. In 1955, for instance, he began buying weapons from the Soviet Union and the following year, he ordered Egyptian soldiers to seize the Suez Canal. By nationalizing the canal, Nasser directly threatened Britain's and Europe's access to oil, most of which traveled through the canal. Through the diplomatic intervention of President Eisenhower, armed conflict was avoided between Great Britain and France on one side and Egypt on the other. Egypt retained control of the canal, a clear victory for Nasser.

Complicating U.S. relations with the Middle East was its support for Israel, which had been established in 1948. As the historian Douglas Little has noted, President Harry S. Truman recognized the new Israeli state only eleven minutes after it was officially founded, not only because he believed it was morally right to do so but also for two other reasons: He depended on the Jewish Democratic vote at home, and he believed that Israel would stand up to the Soviet Union more effectively than would the Arab governments surrounding it. But Truman also became deeply uneasy about Israel's desire for territorial expansion. To the Arab governments in the region, such expansionism was a direct threat to their national borders. Moreover, the establishment of the Israeli state in British-controlled Palestine resulted in the displacement of hundreds of thousands of Palestinians, whose own cause to create a state drew political and financial support from Arab nations. Israelis and Palestinians laid claim to the same land, and their ongoing, violent standoff consistently blew up into major international crises.

U.S. government officials were never naive about the political minefields they navigated, trying to balance U.S. support for Israel with assuring the Arab governments that Washington took their concerns seriously. On the one hand, the United States increasingly saw Israel as a critical bulwark against what appeared to be a rising tide of Arab nationalism and Soviet incursions into the region. Beginning in 1958, the U.S. government anchored that belief by agreeing to sell Israel military arms that presumably could be used in the event of either Arab or Soviet threats. On the other hand, the United States wanted to protect its interests in Saudi oil, knowing that the Saudi rulers felt strong ties to the Palestinian cause and that Arabs across the region laced their anti-Israel politics with a strong dose of anti-Americanism. But this balancing act grew increasingly difficult to maintain. Israel's nuclear ambitions throughout the 1960s, as well as its aggressive rhetoric, military purchases, and continual quest for more land, fueled the support that Arab nationalists and Palestinian activists and terrorists received in the region. The U.S. government and oil executives tried to defend their competing aims in the Middle East by pointing to the fact that U.S. diplomatic relations with Israel were a matter of international relations, whereas Aramco's operations were a private, commercial enterprise. Given the importance of the oil supply and oil revenues to both the Persian Gulf countries and the United States, however, this dividing line would seem increasingly artificial over the years, particularly as American consumers met more of their oil needs with Middle Eastern oil.

Finally, in addition to all the quandaries that Aramco's presence in Saudi Arabia created, this question remained: Did the formation of Aramco indicate a return to what amounted to a monopoly in the American oil industry? Although this question did not concern Americans too much at the time of the founding of Aramco in 1948, eventually it was bound to upset Americans' views of the oil industry. Of course, the Persian Gulf region was not Texas. The countries in the area did not simply throw open their doors to anyone who wanted to drill for oil. But the few companies that did get in the door—such as the companies that made up Aramco, Gulf Oil, and a handful of others—had access to and control over the largest volume of petroleum reserves in the world.

Although the oil exporting countries had managed to work out better financial arrangements for themselves over the course of the 1950s, they also wanted to have a greater role in controlling the oil revenues that came into their governments. By joining together, these countries sought to increase their bargaining power, particularly in the matter of setting prices. The result was the formation of OPEC in 1960. Comprising mostly Arab states, but also including Iran, Venezuela, and, later, Indonesia, Algeria, and Nigeria, the organization hoped that, like the Texas Railroad Commission, it could regulate oil production in order to avoid pumping out too much oil and therefore causing the price to drop. More important, because these countries' revenues depended so much on oil, OPEC now demanded that oil companies consult the organization concerning matters of price generally. Thus a new international entity was born that, by the early 1970s, could stand up to the powerful multinational oil companies around the globe. When that happened, American attention would turn once again to the question of whether corporate power in the oil industry had become too concentrated, especially in the Persian Gulf.

AMERICAN OIL CONSUMPTION AND ENVIRONMENTAL POLITICS

In the two decades that followed the end of World War II, gas was cheap and plentiful in America, as domestic producers largely kept up with rising demand. That fact helped fuel the enormous economic boom that preceded the energy crisis of the early 1970s. Whereas Europe and large parts of Asia lay devastated after the war, the United States made the transition to a peacetime economy relatively easily. But it was a different kind of peace than what Americans had experienced before. Within only a couple of years, U.S. leaders and much of the general public found themselves in a cold war with the nation's wartime ally, the Soviet Union. This conflict entailed both a strategic battle for influence in countries around the world and an ideological battle over which economic and political system created the greatest good. The cold war would produce numerous hot wars—including the Korean War, which began only five years after the end of World War II—but it also contributed to America's economic surge after 1945. Especially in parts of the South and West, private defense contractors built up their operations to manufacture military materiel and produce technology to fight the cold war. The defense industry employed millions of Americans and produced housing booms in cities such as Los Angeles, Seattle, Houston, and Atlanta. Other sectors of American manufacturing also expanded quickly, not only benefiting from the needs of postwar Europe (which the United States helped to rebuild under the 1948 Marshall Plan) but also meeting the consumer demands of Americans.

The automobile was central to this expanding economy and to ordinary Americans' daily lives. Between 1945 and 1960, the number of cars in the United States increased by 133 percent. As government funding went to building roads instead of public transportation (for example, creating the interstate highway system under the Federal Aid Highway Act of 1956), and as white Americans moved in ever greater numbers to the new suburbs, people relied on their cars to get them to work and, in many areas of the country, to the shopping plazas and malls that developers were beginning to build. Cheap gasoline was key to this lifestyle, just as it was to moving consumer goods to market. In fact, over the course of the 1950s and 1960s, so many of those goods—from plastics to fertilizers—were made from petroleum that few aspects of Americans' lives were not touched by the oil industry.

Most people were unaware of the strong links between their daily lives and petroleum in the postwar years. That situation began to change, however, during the tumultuous 1960s.

Americans' awareness of the effects of oil production and consumption on the environment did not arise in a vacuum. The environment had, in fact, been the focus of increasing interest in the United States for decades. Since the late nineteenth century, groups of Americans both in and out of government had organized to protect natural resources from wasteful exploitation. Some conservation leaders had worked to get the government involved in preserving federal land in the West by regulating the cutting of timber. Others had sought to manage water resources in ways that would control floods and provide irrigation for agricultural fields. Some Americans had worked to get the federal government directly involved in managing western grazing lands for ranchers' use. Others had sought government protection of the spectacular landscapes of the West in what would become a system of national parks and wilderness areas.

These efforts at conserving and protecting natural resources, especially land, continued in the postwar years, but other issues emerged that would more substantially shape how Americans began to think about the environment. Environmental historians sometimes label these "quality of life" issues: as many Americans experienced an increasing standard of living after the war, in no small measure due to the cheap price of gasoline, they turned their attention to the rising environmental costs of modern life. Suburbanization—the very process that seemed to better Americans' lives by taking them out of the cities and putting them in new communities of single-family homes and lawns—became the focus of the nascent environmental movement. As thousands of acres of farms and woodlands succumbed to housing developers' bulldozers, local groups began to organize to protect open space. Although their initial efforts often emerged out of a desire to protect scenic landscapes and to keep population pressures at bay, their understanding of the costs of development deepened over time. By the mid- to late 1960s, criticism of suburban sprawl evolved to include widespread evidence that development was producing a variety of environmental threats, from poorer water quality to loss of wildlife habitat.

But suburbanization was not solely to blame for environmental degradation. The spectacular rise of America's gross national product—from $200 billion in 1940 to $500 billion in 1960—indicated that all sectors of the economy were running at full throttle, as factories and farms produced more goods and crops than ever before. Such productivity took a growing toll on nature. Americans noticed this toll in their daily lives, in the form of polluted rivers and manufacturing waste, but it was not until 1962 that environmental problems came to the forefront. That year, biologist Rachel Carson published *Silent Spring,* one of the most important books of the twentieth century. Carson began her book with a chilling scenario of the future, a world in which all the songbirds had perished as a result of toxic chemicals in the environment:

There was a strange stillness. The birds, for example: where had they gone? Many people spoke of them, puzzled and disturbed. The feeding stations in the backyards were deserted. The few birds seen anywhere were moribund; they trembled violently and could not fly. It was spring without voices. On the mornings that had once throbbed with the dawn chorus of robins, catbirds, doves, jays, wrens, and scores of other bird voices there was now no sound; only silence lay over the fields and woods and marsh.[6]

Carson aimed most of her fire at the chemical industry, citing the enormous increase in chemical use by postwar America, not only in industry and agriculture but also in Americans' households. Carson argued that living things simply could not bear the toxic load of chemicals such as the insecticide DDT, which the federal government would later ban, and that chemical scientists and companies had an obligation to address the long-term effects of their products on animals and people. In response, Carson was widely condemned as a hysterical woman, like Chicken Little proclaiming that the sky was falling. And yet her message quickly caught the attention of the American public and government officials. Although Carson died in 1964 from breast cancer, her book helped spark the government's interest in monitoring environmental quality.

Whereas *Silent Spring* tapped into local concerns about the environment, helping to frame them in terms of a national debate, a huge oil spill off the coast of Santa Barbara, California, in 1969 galvanized an increasingly powerful political movement around the environment. Caused by a blowout of an offshore well, in which more than three million gallons of oil washed up on Santa Barbara beaches, the spill provided the environmental movement with potent images of the industrial degradation of nature. News reports of fouled beaches and oil-soaked birds and sea mammals gave visual proof to environmentalists' message that America's juggernaut economy could involve incalculable costs.

While environmentalists framed the blowout within the larger political debate about industrial pollution, the event also focused criticism more specifically on the oil industry and the federal government. As one industry journal noted in 1999, the blowout created "a tectonic shift in the world's attitude toward industry in general [and] the oil industry in particular." It did not help that the head of Union Oil, the company operating the offshore oil platform, responded to the crisis by saying, "I am amazed at the publicity for the loss of a few birds." Public outrage built in the face of such a blithe attitude, and environmentalists successfully used the disaster to expand the message of their movement.[7] Activists also attacked the federal government for its lack of effective mechanisms to deal with the oil spill and for the easy access it provided oil companies to offshore leases controlled by the Department of the Interior. For many environmentalists, the Santa Barbara blowout was yet another instance—and a particularly destructive one—of the government's caving in to industry pressure, and they argued forcefully that Washington needed to protect the public interest more effectively.

Environmentalists' attacks on industrial pollution and government policy reached a high point at the beginning of the 1970s. These years saw a wealth of activism and publication around environmental issues ranging from concerns over world population growth to the future supply of material resources. Although President Richard Nixon had little sympathy for the environmental movement, his Democratic opposition was strong enough that, for political reasons, he could not risk dismissing environmental legislation. His first administration (1969–1973) built on the momentum that had emerged under Lyndon Johnson's presidency to give the federal government new powers to protect environmental quality. In 1970, Nixon signed the National Environmental Policy Act (NEPA), arguably one of the most far-reaching acts in the last third of the twentieth century for the way that it placed the government directly in charge of evaluating and trying to stave off the environmental costs of economic activity. Along with the Clean Air Act of 1970 and the Clear Water Act of 1972 (both having antecedents in earlier, though weaker, legislation in the 1960s), NEPA changed the landscape of American politics, forcing politicians both to take a stand on environmental controversies and to integrate their position into their broader ideological stances.

Environmentalists experienced the peak of their power in the late 1960s and early 1970s, but their political capital began to diminish after Nixon's reelection in 1972. Several reasons explain this demise: the natural ebbing of political power as a movement ages; the changes within the environmental movement itself, as it began to address the ramifications of legislation such as NEPA; and Nixon's own reluctance to press environmental protections very far. But the question of America's future energy supply certainly contributed to the transformation of the environmental debate.

THE OIL CRISIS AND ITS LEGACY

By 1970, it was clear to the Nixon administration and to many in the general public that the balance of world oil production and consumption was shifting quite rapidly. The problem in a nutshell: Americans

were consuming oil at ever greater rates, while the country was producing diminishing quantities of oil domestically. For ten years, the
United States had had in place oil import quotas to keep foreign oil to
a minimum and give an advantage to domestically produced oil. But as
consumer demand surged and oil supplies at home began to decrease,
Nixon called for a task force to reevaluate the quota policy. Meanwhile, the administration also pushed to open Alaska's North Slope to
oil development after exploration there confirmed that upwards of
10 billion barrels of oil lay underground. (To put this estimate in perspective, in the same years Saudi Arabian reserves were estimated at
150 billion barrels, and that estimate has increased substantially in the
decades since.) A remote region of northern Alaska, bounded by the
Arctic Sea, the North Slope became a political battleground for American environmentalists who wanted to protect it from resource development. Building on public hostility to the oil industry after the Santa
Barbara oil spill, environmental organizations challenged oil companies' plans for drilling and especially for laying an eight-hundred-mile
pipeline to transport oil from Prudhoe Bay in the north to the port of
Valdez, where it could then be shipped by tanker to the lower forty-
eight states. With the passage of NEPA, statutory regulations raised
more barriers that environmental organizations used for a time to
block Alaskan oil development. Native groups within the state also
fought in the courts and the halls of Congress to have the government
and the oil industry take seriously their land rights in the area proposed for development.

The fight for Alaska was an especially critical battle for environmentalists. On the one hand, they skillfully used NEPA to force the oil
industry and the government to address the myriad environmental
problems that would result from the production and transportation of
oil in Alaska. On the other hand, they did not manage to save the
North Slope—called "the last great frontier" by environmentalists—
from development. Perhaps more important, the emerging energy crisis
undermined environmentalists' arguments about the value of preser-
vation over resource development. As concerns grew over the decreas-
ing supplies of domestically produced oil, Nixon and other supporters
of the Alaska pipeline argued that opening Alaska to oil production
would substantially lessen America's dependence on foreign oil.

This was an appealing argument. When Nixon ended the oil import
quota program in the spring of 1973, and as Congress still battled over
the question of the Alaska pipeline, the United States was clearly heading down a path where it would increasingly rely on foreign oil, particularly from the Persian Gulf region. By this point, in the words of

State Department energy specialist James Akins, "the wolf [was] here" (Document 5). Americans needed to grasp that their domestic industry could never keep up with their demands and that without changing course — such as developing alternative energy sources and reducing consumption — the United States faced the political and economic dangers of relying too much on Middle Eastern oil (see map). As the documents in the pages that follow make clear, Akins was not the only one who saw danger on the horizon. The Nixon administration was just the latest in a chain of presidential administrations to struggle with the Arab-Israeli question. Well aware of Arab anger at Israel's expansionist moves into both Palestinian lands and neighboring countries, and deeply concerned over Israel's nuclear ambitions, Nixon nonetheless believed — like the postwar presidents before him — that supporting Israel would counter Soviet inroads in the region.

Israel's military aggressiveness was a constant target of Arab protest and terrorism. OPEC joined the political battle when it attempted to impose an oil embargo in 1967 in response to Israel's attack on Egypt. This first embargo was unsuccessful, in large part because the supply of oil worldwide was large enough to create a buyer's market that benefited oil consuming countries more than oil producing ones. But in the following years, the organization began dealing with oil companies much more aggressively than it had before. At the same time, the world economic climate was changing. In the early 1970s, the value of the American dollar fell dramatically, and since Middle Eastern oil was sold in dollars on the world market, the oil exporting countries were receiving less and less revenue. Therefore, they had an even greater interest in seeing an increase in the price of oil.

The precise concerns that Akins imagined, such as OPEC's determination to raise prices or enact an embargo as political retaliation,

---

Map of Major Oil Fields and Pipelines in the Middle East, 1972
Although it took the oil crisis of 1973–1974 to force Americans to confront their growing dependence on Middle East oil, the petroleum industry had a sustained presence in the region that dated back to the early twentieth century. Before World War II, the British developed the oilfields in southwest Iran, while a consortium of British, European, and American companies — known as the Iraq Petroleum Company — struck oil in Iraq. After World War II, American companies dominated new oil exploration and production in the Persian Gulf. In 1959, oil was struck in Libya, which granted numerous concessions to different oil companies and which quickly emerged as a major oil exporter, especially to European countries.

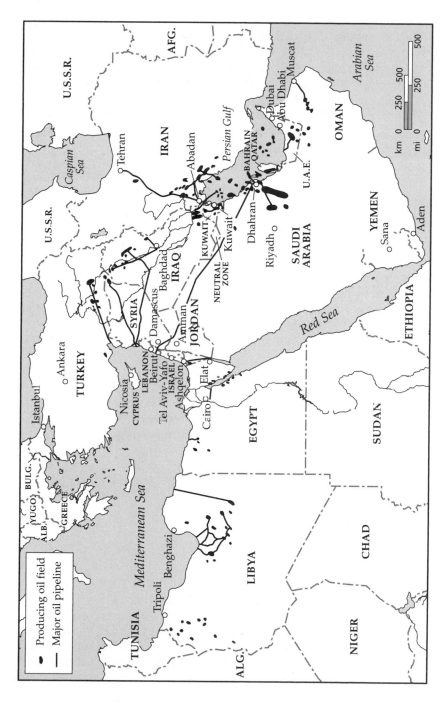

became a reality in 1973. In October of that year, Nixon agreed to provide more Phantom jets to Israel after the surprise attack by Egypt
and Syria in what would become known as the Yom Kippur War.
Overnight, OPEC raised the price of its oil from $3 to $5.11 per barrel, and on October 19 the Arab states within the organization decided to cut off oil entirely to the United States. As winter approached
and U.S. energy demands correspondingly increased, OPEC continued to raise the price of oil. By January 1974, a barrel of oil cost more
than $11—almost four times the price it had been just three months
earlier.

From the perspective of the Arab countries, these policies had clear
goals: to change America's pro-Israel stance and force the United
States to discontinue sales of military armaments to Israel; to force
Israel to retreat from its territorial ambitions; to build international
support for the Palestinian cause; and to pressure other countries that
were more dependent on Arab oil than the United States to back Arab
positions in their foreign policy. However, such clarity in their goals
did not mean that the Arab members of OPEC reached a consensus
about the use of the embargo as a political weapon. Divisions between
them marked the six-month period between October 1973 and March
1974, especially as the United States became a central player in working out the terms of Egyptian-Israeli disengagement in the wake of the
Yom Kippur War. Some OPEC countries, such as Saudi Arabia, wanted
to link the lifting of the embargo to American diplomatic efforts in the
disengagement negotiations, but others, such as Libya, believed that
the embargo should be continued despite these efforts. Assured that
Israel would withdraw from the contested territory, the Arab members
of OPEC voted in March 1974 to end the embargo. But they looked
forward to having a continuing and more forceful economic role in the
world oil market.

For many countries in the world, particularly those with large Muslim populations, the Arab use of the oil weapon was a watershed event,
proving that the United States' increasing dependence on foreign oil
was a significant threat to its maintaining a hegemonic presence in
international politics. For many Americans, that message was both
economically painful and politically devastating. In the winter of
1973–1974, public outrage and commentary on the oil crisis flew off
the pages of newspapers and magazines and sounded in congressional
hearings. Every angle of the crisis was analyzed. What remains strik-
ing in hindsight is the depth and complexity of the self-scrutiny that
many Americans undertook to grasp what had happened. This

scrutiny no doubt was enhanced by the fact that U.S. involvement in the Vietnam War had just ended and the nation was gripped by the emerging Watergate scandal. The oil crisis clarified people's understanding of two powerful features of America's place in the postwar world: the environmental costs of the nation's rise to economic power, and the political conundrums that arose out of America's enormous resource needs, particularly the country's increasing dependence on foreign oil.

Not surprisingly, no consensus ever emerged about what the country should do to address these issues, and the nationwide conversation about oil continued long after the embargo officially ended. Clear patterns began to emerge in the wake of the crisis, however. There was virtual agreement among Americans of all political stripes that the United States was relying too much on oil from other countries, especially those represented in OPEC. The trends were startling: Whereas the United States drew 19 percent of its oil from foreign sources in 1967, that number had increased to 36 percent by 1975.[8] It was also clear that existing oil operations in this country could no longer meet the growing consumer demand for petroleum products.

Proposed solutions to these problems began emerging from the White House and Congress almost immediately, as the energy crisis consumed politicians' attention and created great enthusiasm for imagining how the United States could achieve energy independence. Throughout the 1970s, while OPEC continued to post high prices for its crude oil, Democrats and Republicans agreed that the United States needed to conserve energy better. In 1975, Congress passed the Energy Policy and Conservation Act, which established for the first time fuel efficiency standards for automobiles—the Corporate Average Fuel Economy (CAFE) standards. The American automobile industry responded by producing smaller, more fuel-efficient cars, although automakers faced stiff competition from Japanese and German manufacturers, which had been producing such cars for some time. The act also helped spur industry to manufacture more fuel-conserving products, such as more efficient appliances and better insulation for buildings. Finally, Congress authorized the government to buy oil that would fill the Strategic Petroleum Reserve. This oil could be used in case of an emergency in which exporting countries cut off supplies entirely from the United States.

How much more should the government do? Americans were deeply divided over that question. Most Democrats, especially those sympathetic with environmentalists, believed that the federal government should gather both its regulatory and monetary resources to overhaul the country's dependence on petroleum in particular and fossil fuels in general. Electric cars, solar-powered homes, and wind farms were some alternative forms of energy that the government might foster to create true energy independence. But Democrats were divided over the government's role in promoting other forms of domestic energy production that were not so environmentally friendly, such as nuclear power and coal. Democratic President Jimmy Carter embraced the importance of energy conservation but also pushed to build more nuclear power plants and open up more coalfields. He also launched ill-fated programs to try to produce synthetic oil and to extract oil from shale.

Most Republicans pushed for more exploration and development of fossil fuels domestically. Enthusiastic about the opening of Alaska's North Slope to drilling and about the building of the Trans-Alaska Pipeline, they hoped to make it easier for oil operators to obtain leases on federal lands in the western lower forty-eight states as well. But Republicans also were deeply divided—and in constant disagreement with Democrats—over what course the federal government should take to intervene in the oil market. All three presidents during the 1970s—Richard Nixon, Gerald Ford, and Jimmy Carter—oversaw complicated price controls on oil, and Ford even suggested taxing imported oil. But this idea never achieved broad support among either Republicans or Democrats.

The tone and substance of these debates were transformed with the arrival of Ronald Reagan in the White House in 1981. Dedicated to reducing the scope of federal government activity, Reagan quickly deregulated oil prices, arguing that the market would eventually bring prices to an appropriate level. He also tried to abolish the Department of Energy, which had been established in 1977 during the Carter administration. While this latter proposal proved unsuccessful, the move indicated that throughout the 1980s, energy would no longer occupy Washington's full attention either as an economic or as an environmental issue.

This shift did not mean that Reagan ignored the energy issue entirely. In fact, with oil imports still rising, Reagan continued the course set by his predecessor to bring a greater American military presence to the Persian Gulf. Following the Islamic revolution in Iran in 1979, in which fifty-two Americans were held hostage and the U.S. embassy was seized, President Carter had announced boldly in his 1980 State of the Union address, "Let our position be absolutely clear:

An attempt by any outside force to gain control of the Persian Gulf region will be regarded as an assault on the vital interests of the United States of America, and such an assault will be repelled by any means necessary, including military force." This declaration, which became known as the Carter Doctrine (Document 28), represented a true watershed in America's stance toward the Middle East, ratcheting up the country's commitment to protect its interests in securing oil. But this more aggressive position was not implemented until the Reagan administration. In 1983, United States Central Command, or CENTCOM, was established in Tampa, Florida. The fifth of the Defense Department's unified command centers, which coordinate U.S. combat forces around the world, CENTCOM became responsible for all the countries around the Persian Gulf, as well as those in Southwest Asia and the Horn of Africa. CENTCOM has since overseen combat forces in three wars: the Persian Gulf War of 1991, the war in Afghanistan (2001), and the war in Iraq (2003).

Thus Reagan launched the U.S. government in two directions that differed dramatically from the politics of oil in the 1970s. First, he declared that the government had little responsibility in setting long-term energy policy and should not try to tinker with oil prices. He and other conservatives believed that the market would direct our energy choices in ways that would bring supply and demand into better balance, allow for new investment in the oil industry, and ultimately meet American consumers' needs. These beliefs were, of course, in keeping with conservative economic ideas that sought to lessen or remove government regulations from business and reduce government spending on domestic programs. Among other things, Reagan cut the federal government's regulatory oversight of and spending on environmental programs. Second, Reagan believed that no cost was too great for American defense, especially against the Soviet Union and Soviet influence in countries around the world. In this sense, his administration's launching of CENTCOM fit neatly within the newly empowered conservative view that a greater military presence in the Persian Gulf would secure U.S. national interests, not only in terms of America's access to oil but also in projecting a strong military presence in an area that the Soviets also saw as strategically important.

With the fall of the Berlin Wall in 1989 and the subsequent disintegration of the Soviet Union, the cold war no longer dominated Washington's global concerns. With the crash in oil prices in 1986—due in part to reduced American demand, which was the consequence of greater energy efficiency—OPEC faced the end of the twentieth century with little of the political power it had enjoyed during the 1970s. Indeed, with very cheap gasoline available in the 1990s, America saw the rise of the gas-guzzling sport-utility vehicle (SUV), which symbolized to many the public's repudiation of 1970s thinking. Whereas car manufacturers in the post-embargo years had proclaimed the virtue of fuel economy in their advertisements, now they proclaimed the virtues of size and power. Despite the growing scientific conviction that the world's hydrocarbon age was producing global climate change, the consumption of oil in the United States increased throughout the 1990s, due primarily to dramatic increases in transportation's share of oil consumption near the end of the decade. Foreign oil imports, including oil from the Persian Gulf region, rose to meet the demand. By 2005, the United States was importing close to 60 percent of its oil.

CONCLUSION

In the decades that followed the oil crisis, conflict continued to emerge out of America's position toward the Middle East in general and the Arab oil producing countries specifically. Not all of that conflict has been about America's need for oil. Other strategic and diplomatic concerns have driven the U.S. government to secure a permanent military presence in the region. But as the United States grows even more dependent on Middle Eastern oil, especially on that from Saudi Arabia (the third-largest source of imported oil in America after Canada and Venezuela), oil continues to play a prominent role in dictating U.S. policy toward the Middle East more than three decades after the oil crisis.

By 2006, the national discussion over oil dependence sounded quite similar to that of the early 1970s. Many conservatives, including President George W. Bush, argued that the United States must engage in an all-out push to produce oil and natural gas domestically. Bush strongly supported opening up the Arctic National Wildlife Refuge, just east of the North Slope oil fields, to drilling. Others opposed such a move, arguing that successful drilling there would recover only enough oil to keep America running for about six months—not enough to justify the risk of destroying that fragile landscape.

More than three decades after the OPEC embargo, amid increased prices at the pump and concerns about the political stability of the Middle East, many leaders across the political spectrum renewed calls for energy independence. Although this phrase harks back to the 1973–1974 oil crisis, it is a malleable term. For some, it calls up the twin concerns of the early 1970s: (1) that high levels of American oil consumption result in dangerous environmental costs—particularly climate change, the science of which was in its infancy during the first oil shock—and (2) that our dependence on oil produced in countries controlled by autocratic and potentially unstable regimes (such as Saudi Arabia) threatens our national security. For many Americans, the fact that the United States still struggled with these issues in 2006 indicated that it had not learned the lessons of the 1973–1974 oil crisis. For some, those lessons revolved around the need for the U.S. government to reduce America's dependence on petroleum by finding alternative energy sources. For others, the lesson was that America needed to expand and secure its access to oil by encouraging exploration and drilling at home and abroad and by establishing a strong military presence in the region with the greatest oil reserves, the Persian Gulf.

Both of these views, while seemingly different on the surface, share the same belief that the United States can achieve a certain level of independence in its reliance on petroleum. But such an assumption ignores the profound ways in which the use of oil in the modern world is a product of *interdependence*. Americans, like many people throughout the world, are dependent on an international array of people, machinery, and processes that provide them with the gas they put in their tanks. Moreover, as with all other natural resources, people are fundamentally dependent on the planet itself. The fact is that oil is a finite resource distributed very unevenly around the world. The passage of time since the 1973–1974 oil crisis has likely altered many Americans' visions of what lies ahead. But as oil supplies slowly diminish, this "black gold" will undoubtedly continue to be the source of national and international debate.

NOTES

[1] "The New Highway Guerrillas," *Time*, December 17, 1973, 33.

[2] The Arab countries of OPEC also placed an embargo against the Netherlands for its support of Israel in this war, which is known as the Yom Kippur War.

[3] Robert Brenner, *The Boom and the Bubble: The U.S. in the World Economy* (London: Verso, 2002), 18.

[4]The word *imperium* comes from the title of chapter 31 in Daniel Yergin's book *The Prize: The Epic Quest for Oil, Money, and Power* (New York: Simon and Schuster, 1991).

[5]That journalist was Ludwell Denny, who wrote *We Fight for Oil* (1928; reprint, New York: Hyperion Press, 1976).

[6]Rachel Carson, *Silent Spring* (1962; reprint, Boston: Houghton Mifflin, 1992), 1–2.

[7]"Another Day That Lives in Infamy," *Explorer* (American Association of Petroleum Geologists newsletter), June 2003, http://64.233.161.104/search?q=cache :ePDEliKMhoEJ:www.aapg.org/explorer/2003/06jun.

[8]Yergin, *The Prize*, 567.

For further citations to books and articles used in the writing of this introduction, see the selected bibliography on pages 163–65.

PART TWO

The Documents

1

The United States and the Middle East before the Crisis

The acronym OPEC became part of the American political vocabulary during 1973, but the Organization of Petroleum Exporting Countries had quietly existed since 1960. The organization was formed in response to decades of frustration felt by oil exporting nations in dealing with foreign oil companies. The major oil companies operating in these nations controlled the pricing of their product, and although most of the exporting countries had successfully fought for a greater share of the profits, their revenues depended on a price structure over which they had no influence. When the supply was tight and the price was high, the exporting nations enjoyed a steady income. But when the supply exceeded the demand and the majors dropped their prices, the countries saw a sudden reduction in revenues. This occurred at the end of the 1950s, sparking the emergence of what writer Joe Stork has labeled an "oil consciousness" among exporting countries, especially in the Persian Gulf region. This consciousness brought to many people in these countries "an awareness of the strategic and economic value of Middle East oil to the West; of the mechanisms of corporate power and control over the producing countries; and of the amount of waste and exploitation that characterized the industry in its squandering of irreplaceable natural wealth."[1]

As the following documents show, the U.S. government did not foresee the importance of OPEC's formation, but the majors did, particularly Aramco. If the exporting countries could work together, they posed a threat to the oil companies' control over how they priced oil and how much they produced. But OPEC was not the only source of the majors' anxiety in the 1960s. Equally troubling was the "frightening erosion of the American position in the area," as Henry Moses,

[1]Joe Stork, *Middle East Oil and the Energy Crisis* (New York: Monthly Review Press, 1975), 88.

vice president of Mobil Oil, put it, due to U.S. support for Israel, especially after the Six-Day War in 1967 (Document 2). Israel made territorial gains in the war, which escalated Arab protests against both Israel and the United States. Moses worried that these protests "might even engulf Aramco."

Anti-American sentiment did not engulf Aramco at that moment, but during the early 1970s the Persian Gulf nations would take the lead in turning OPEC into an international political player. By all estimates, these countries contained more oil reserves than any other part of the world. Although they provided the United States with only about 15 percent of its oil imports, that figure was expected to rise with each coming year. Compared to its economic position in the 1960s, OPEC found itself in a classic seller's market, which afforded the organization opportunities to change the balance of power between member countries and the major oil companies.

1

The U.S. Government and the Oil Industry React to the Formation of OPEC

1960

Although the oil crisis would not explode until late 1973, it would never have unfolded in the way that it did without the formation of OPEC thirteen years earlier. Excerpts from three documents detail the U.S. government's and the oil industry's initial reactions to OPEC. Unlike government officials, the oil companies were clearly concerned about this new player in the oil game.

Telegram from the Embassy in Iraq
to the Department of State

September 15, 1960

A telegram to the U.S. State Department from the American embassy in Baghdad, Iraq, reported straightforwardly about the formation of OPEC in September 1960.

Conference five oil producing states ended September 14 after agreeing establish permanent body called Organization Petroleum Exporting Countries. Baghdad conferees are founding members, but OPEC open to "any country which exports large quantity crude oil." Conference also set up Secretariat for OPEC and directed it prepare agenda, rules, and documentation for second meeting scheduled for January in Caracas. OPEC expecting carry out regular consultations with members to coordinate and unify their policies and determine line be followed in future "emergencies."

According press producing states decided they must voice their objections to attitudes shown by oil companies in reducing prices recently and call upon companies maintain fixed stable prices. Conference also decided producing states should take all possible steps restore crude prices to level prevailing before recent cuts and agreed participants should study measures be taken ensure stable prices in future. Official announcement decisions conference will be released simultaneously September 24 in all capitals participants.

Press commented conference decisions stemmed from realization by producers that their development programs dependent on oil revenues and that "any fluctuations in oil prices will halt economic development in oil producing and exporting countries" as well as affect economies oil consuming nations. [Government of Iraq Minister of Oil] in public statement declared producing states not seeking anything which might harm either companies or consumers. "Our cause just and we not demanding anything which unjust." Prior departure all delegates expressed complete satisfaction with accomplishments conference.

"Telegram from the Embassy in Iraq to the Department of State," in *Foreign Relations of the United States, 1958–1960*, vol. XII, *Near East Region; Iraq; Iran; Arabian Peninsula* (Washington, D.C.: Government Printing Office, 1993), 274.

Memorandum of Discussion at the 460th Meeting of the National Security Council

September 21, 1960

The lack of outward concern expressed in the previous telegram is echoed in this summary of a discussion a week later by the National Security Council, which included President Dwight Eisenhower, his special assistant for national security affairs Gordon Gray, and CIA director Allen Dulles. The council's main concerns about OPEC revolved around the role of Egypt, because of its nationalist and Soviet-leaning president, Gamal Abdel Nasser. After taking part in a military coup in 1952, Nasser came to power in 1954 and proved to be an extraordinarily popular leader among Arabs in the Middle East, primarily because he stood up to the Western powers under the banner of Pan-Arabism — the belief that the Arab countries should join together as a politically unified force. As is evident from this summary, Egypt played no role in OPEC because it contained little oil.

Mr. Gray introduced the subject to the Council. . . .

At the conclusion of Mr. Gray's presentation, the President said he had received the most glowing reports on the prospects for petroleum production in Libya. He had been told that the Libyan reserves exceeded even the Sahara reserves. He asked whether Mr. Gray had available an estimate of possible oil production in Libya. Mr. Dulles remarked that the latest estimates on Libyan oil production were not quite as optimistic as the estimates which were current a year ago. The President said reports he had received indicated that Libya had a great oil field and would receive huge amounts of money from oil production. . . .

Mr. Gray then reported on the formation last week of the new Organization of Petroleum Exporting Countries, with Saudi Arabia, Iraq, Iran, Kuwait, and Venezuela as members. The purpose of the Organization was to control production and prices. What impact it will

---

"Memorandum of Discussion at the 460th Meeting of the National Security Council," in *Foreign Relations of the United States, 1958–1960*, vol. XII, *Near East Region; Iraq; Iran; Arabian Peninsula* (Washington, D.C.: Government Printing Office, 1993), 275–76.

have on the world oil picture remains to be seen. The President said that as far as the Middle Eastern countries in the new Organization were concerned, anyone could break up the Organization by offering five cents more per barrel for the oil of one of the countries. Mr. Dulles said that the five countries represented 80 per cent of the oil reserves in the world and half of the oil in world trade. Egypt had not been invited to be a member of this Organization because it was thought Egypt would not collaborate with Iran due to Iranian-Egyptian tension over Israel. The President said he thought Egypt had no oil in any case. Mr. Dulles agreed that Egypt had very little oil; however, the country was interested in oil questions because of the Syrian pipelines. He said that Venezuela intended to seek Soviet cooperation with the OPEC, taking the line that Soviet price cuts will hurt the underdeveloped countries. Secretary Dillon thought this Venezuelan initiative would be helpful. It had been demonstrated in the past that the USSR was responsive to protests from underdeveloped countries.

Memorandum of Conversation: Standard Oil Company (New Jersey) Views on the Organization of Petroleum Exporting Countries

October 19, 1960

The month after the formation of OPEC, executives from Standard Oil of New Jersey, one of the companies involved in Saudi oil operations, talked with representatives of the U.S. State Department about the new petroleum organization. In contrast to the government officials cited in the previous two sources, American oil companies doing business in the Middle East were very concerned about how OPEC would affect the oil industry.

The Jersey company representatives called at their own request to discuss problems resulting from the formation of the Organization of Petroleum Exporting Countries (OPEC).

"Memorandum of Conversation," in *Foreign Relations of the United States, 1958–1960*, vol. XII, *Near East Region; Iraq; Iran; Arabian Peninsula* (Washington, D.C.: Government Printing Office, 1993), 277–79.

Mr. Welch[1] stated that the Jersey company is greatly concerned about the implications for the oil industry and the security position of the West resulting from the formation of OPEC. He fears that the companies will be caught between producer country controls and the demands of consuming countries. They will no longer be able to manage their business in a normal way since the governments would take over the determination of oil prices, the amounts of oil to be produced, and the destination of oil shipments.

The Jersey representatives believe a sharp distinction should be drawn between prorationing[2] in Texas and the international prorationing scheme proposed by OPEC. They also believe that experience with other commodities is not pertinent in determining whether an international oil agreement is feasible or desirable. . . .

Jersey thinks that progress can be made with the Arabs by talking oil economics. They would urge the Arabs not to go too fast in OPEC without knowing what the consequences may be. The companies can show the Arabs that they have not been hurt by the present concessional system or by the recent price cuts; there has been no reduction in national revenues from oil, and increases in world demand should protect governments against future loss of revenues. OPEC on the other hand might hold production back, for example in Iran, Iraq, and Kuwait, without offering certainty of higher prices to compensate for it. Moreover, the companies can point out that if a bloc of powerful consuming countries is formed and new oil and energy sources are tapped, the OPEC countries would be hurt. . . .

Mr. Welch stated that he hoped the U.S. Government would use its influence in urging the OPEC countries to go slowly in completing the OPEC organization and implementing its program. He said that the United States obviously cannot say that it opposes OPEC, but he did think that the U.S. Government could express the hope that the OPEC countries would consider fully the economic factors involved in their program and would not reach hasty decisions.

Mr. Welch said that he understood that the U.K. Government was opposed to the formation of OPEC and is believed to be approaching Iran regarding it.

---

[1]*Mr. Welch*: Leo Welch, Chairman of the Board, Standard Oil Company (New Jersey). [Ed.]

[2]*prorationing*: limiting the production of oil, either by a government agency or by collective agreement among producers. [Ed.]

Mr. Dillon expressed appreciation on behalf of the Department for Jersey's views on the OPEC.[3]

[3]The following sentence was originally in the memorandum, but was crossed out and replaced by the paragraph as printed: "Mr. Dillon indicated interest in the suggestion that the United States might discreetly attempt to discourage certain countries, particularly Iran, from going ahead with its membership in OPEC, but did not indicate whether or not the U.S. Government would take any action."

2

HENRY MOSES

Situation in the Middle East

October 27, 1969

By the time President Richard Nixon took office in 1969, it was clear that oil and the Middle East would demand the government's attention. Following Israel's capturing of Egyptian land in the Six-Day War of 1967, the Arab countries increased their criticism of American support for Israel, and American oilmen grew anxious about the effects of anti-Americanism within the oil producing nations of the Middle East. In this memo, Henry Moses, vice president of Mobil Oil, described a recent trip to the Middle East, laying out points of concern that he and other oil executives would discuss the following day with Nixon aide Elliot Richardson about the position of the U.S. government in the region.

On the basis of our recent trip to the Middle East we wish to report our first-hand observation of the frightening erosion of the American position in the area to a point where we feel that anti-American sentiment has put in serious jeopardy vital U.S. interests and investments.

As representatives of an industry which in large measure supplies the energy needs of the free world and which returns close to $2 billion

Henry Moses, "Situation in the Middle East," Oil Box 1, Folder 46, John J. McCloy Papers, Amherst College Library, Amherst, Mass.

to the U.S. balance of payments from our operations in the Middle East, we wanted to come in this morning to share with you our observations which grow out of our recent visit in Beirut and Dhahran [Saudi Arabia].

The growth of anti-American sentiment results from many factors:

1. A feeling that the [U.S. government] is the primary supporter of Israel. . . .
2. Frustration over Arab inability to achieve a political solution to the June 1967 war and therefore Israeli withdrawal from occupied Arab territories.
3. Escalation of Israeli retaliatory attacks, such as the raid on the Beirut airport and deep aerial penetration of Jordan as well as ground raids in the U.A.R.[1]
4. The delivery of [P]hantom jets to Israel at the very time that government is engaging in what in Arab eyes are acts of aggression. . . .
6. As a result of all these factors the growing strength of militants . . . throughout the Arab world who operate with few responsibilities but who look toward an important future role in a realigned Middle East power structure.
7. The shift in emphasis by these militants to a positive policy of trying to get the U.S. out of the area, which brings with it a rapidly increasing threat to American installations and personnel in the area. Responsible Arabs told us that the radical commando leadership has resolved to attack American personnel, rather than facilities, in order more speedily to achieve complete withdrawal of the U.S. from the area.
8. Two of us who are members of the Iraq Petroleum Company[2] even see evidence that our British, French and Dutch partners are so concerned about the deteriorating American position that they are reluctant to see Americans participate in any negotiations in Baghdad. If a representative of our companies is to participate it will be a person of non-U.S. birth. European oil companies and governments could indeed

---

[1] *U.A.R.*: United Arab Republic, which was the state founded when Egypt and Syria joined together in 1958. Syria seceded in 1961, but Egypt kept the name until 1971. [Ed.]

[2] *Iraq Petroleum Company*: The Iraq Petroleum Company was a consortium of oil companies that joined together in 1912 and was known as the Turkish Petroleum Company until it changed its name in 1929. Consisting of European and American oil companies, the I.P.C. developed oilfields in northern Iraq. [Ed.]

become so concerned about the U.S. position that they might for reasons of self-preservation attempt to extricate themselves from some of the vital oil relationships in which we are now their partners, and regardless of the damage this may cause to U.S. companies.

9. Increasing Communist penetration in the Middle East which polarizes Arab governments away from the U.S.

The situation has reached the point today where, based on our recent observations, moderate regimes remaining in the area are threatened with revolutionary forces, the main root of which lies in American attitudes toward the Arab/Israeli conflict. King Faisal [Saudi Arabia] in particular is isolated and embarrassed by his consistent advocacy of a pro-American policy. In his traditional address presenting the new Saudi budget Faisal included this year a direct attack on President Nixon's statement to the [UN] General Assembly—the first time in our knowledge that a Saudi monarch has directly criticized an American President.

King Hussein [Jordan], for his consistent moderate and pro-Western stance, is also today virtually under a state of siege. His Foreign Minister, in addressing the General Assembly this fall, included praise for the "freedom fighters" in Vietnam—an obvious slap at the U.S. and one of the few occasions on which Jordan has challenged U.S. policy outside the Middle East.

... The Saudi Arabian Minister of Petroleum told us two weeks ago that anti-American sentiment had so increased that it might even engulf Aramco. As a Beirut editorial typically commented the other day, "relations with the United States range between breach and despair."

In this situation we feel that the prospects for our continued operations in the area are seriously jeopardized. Unfortunately, attitudes toward American firms tend eventually to be related to attitudes toward the United States Government. What we feel is needed today is:

a. An even-handed policy that is in fact even-handed and one that can reasonably be so interpreted within the Arab world.
b. Some expression of concern for the sovereignty, integrity and development of *all* the states in the area, specifically referring to Arab countries as well as Israel.
c. A visit by a senior government official to the Arab states.
d. Recognition that further polarization of the situation in the Middle East can only lead to the ultimate downfall of Israel.
e. A new pragmatic recognition of vital U.S. commercial and

security interests in the Arab Middle East which is balanced with a policy of aid and sympathetic support for Israel.

It is difficult to over-dramatize the urgency of these problems, and the immediate need for a reappraisal and new enunciation of U.S. policy in the area.

3

U.S. NEWS AND WORLD REPORT

The Changing Geopolitics of the World's Oil

April 14, 1969

Henry Moses's sense of the growing "urgency" of Arab anti-Americanism would turn out to be very prescient. In contrast, an article from U.S. News and World Report from the spring of 1969, excerpted here, saw a new geopolitics of world oil production, one in which the United States would decrease its dependence on Middle Eastern oil. Eventually, Alaskan oil reduced America's reliance on foreign imports, at least temporarily. But the amount of oil produced in Alaska has paled in comparison to that from the Persian Gulf.

Sweeping changes under way in the world's oil picture suddenly are shifting the international power balance in the direction of the U.S.

America now is becoming self-sufficient once again in oil, the major source of energy for modern industry and for defense.

Soviet Russia, pinched by rising costs at home, may have to begin importing oil.

Oil finds in Africa, South America, North America and the Middle East are about to provide Western Europe and Japan with new sources of energy—but these nations still remain basically dependent on the U.S. for help in future political crises.

"The Changing Geopolitics of the World's Oil," *U.S. News and World Report*, April 14, 1969, 98.

Exploration for oil is expected to shift more and more to the Arctic and to politically stable areas—away from the Middle East.

Canada and the U.S. are being pulled closer and closer together. . . .

It all adds up to the most dramatic shift in oil's impact on geopolitics since the Middle East became the world's No. 1 oil region in the 1940s.

"What is going on today will turn the power politics of the world upside down," is the way the current situation is summed up by one man who has served in high positions in both the U.S. Government and the oil industry.

For that reason alone, world oil changes shaping up are of major importance in the Nixon Administration's reassessment of American strength and commitments in the world.

And oil will play a part in U.S. strategy in big-power discussions aimed at achieving peace between Israel and the Arabs.

Talks by staff members of "U.S. News & World Report" with diplomats, economists, oil experts and other authorities in the U.S., Canada, Latin America, Europe and other parts of the world show what the changes mean.

The single most important event today, the authorities agree, is discovery of oil on Alaska's Arctic coast. Although exact size of the oil deposits still is not certain, experts now are assuming enough oil is there to keep the U.S. self-sufficient in reasonably priced fuel for the foreseeable future.

Significance of that to diplomats and military men: The U.S. no longer faces the immediate prospect of having to rely on the erratic Middle East for large supplies of petroleum.

That is a bedrock advantage for a world power. The U.S. thus can pursue a more independent policy in defense and international affairs. Russian domination of the Mideast, a growing danger, seems a less catastrophic prospect to the U.S. than formerly.

4

Report of OPEC Meeting with
Oil Company Executives

January 21, 1972

By the early 1970s, OPEC had already been asserting itself more force-fully with the American and British companies doing business in mem-ber nations. Initiated by a revolutionary government in Libya, this new assertiveness produced significant gains for OPEC during 1970 and 1971, when negotiations in Tripoli and Tehran gave the organization a greater say in setting prices. Moreover, OPEC nations developed an increasingly powerful belief that their inherent sovereignty over the oil beneath the ground afforded them more rights than the oil companies had given them. This document, an excerpt from a transcript of a meet-ing between OPEC officials and oil executives in 1972, indicates the changing priorities among the oil exporting nations. No longer con-cerned simply with getting more royalties or being assured that employees from their own countries would receive better job training, OPEC offi-cials now sought greater "participation"—that is, a greater share of the actual ownership (or "equity capital") of oil operations. A. Z. Yamani, minister of oil from Saudi Arabia, represented OPEC's new assertiveness by using a confrontational manner with the oil executives. He argued that OPEC's proposal to increase each country's "share in the equity cap-ital of . . . existing concessions" was an alternative to nationalizing the oil industry within the member states, and he believed that the compa-nies would prefer such an option. Their responses clearly indicated their deep apprehension and even anger about changing existing relations.

Present:
C. J. Hedlund (Esso)
H. C. Moses (Mobil)
A. C. DeCrane (Texaco)
J. W. Simmons (Atlantic Richfield)
W. J. McQuinn (Socal)

"Report of Meeting Held in Geneva at Intercontinental Hotel," Oil Box 1, Folder 46, John J. McCloy Papers, Amherst College Library, Amherst, Mass.

J. O'Brien (Socal)
F. Jungers (Aramco)
A. R. Martin (Gulf)
J. W. R. Sutcliffe (BP)
A. J. Miller (Shell)
A. Manson [Iranian Oil Participants, Ltd.]
J. E. J. Danner [Total Oil]
R. E. R. Bird [Iraq Petroleum Company (IPC)]

Mana Saeed Otaiba (Abu Dhabi)
Mahmoud Hamra-Krouha (Algeria)
A. Z. Yamani (Saudi Arabia)
Saud al-Faisal (Saudi Arabia)
Rashid Al-Rifai (Iraq)
Abdul-Rahman Al-Ateegy (Kuwait)
Shetima Ali Monguno (Nigeria)
Hassan Kamel (Qatar)
Ali Jaida (Qatar)
José Manuel de los Rios (Venezuela)
Dr. Manscer Frouzan (Iran)
Mohammed Sadiq Mahdi (OPEC—Economics Dept.)
Macia (OPEC—Technical Dept.)

Yamani: I would like to welcome you to this very important round of negotiations. Yesterday we were able to solve one important problem and, as George Piercy[1] said, this shows the ability of the countries and the companies to resolve difficult issues. Today's subject, the participation issue, is far more important. We wish to discuss effective implementation of participation.

Sutcliffe: Thank you for your welcome. . . . I would like to emphasize that we are not a team but are here as individuals representing our own companies. I am not in any sense a leader or a spokesman and I am authorized by BP only. This goes for all the oil company representatives.

Moses: When I speak, I speak for Mobil only.

Yamani: This makes it difficult. We want to make a deal with the oil companies. When we have agreed to the principles, the details would be for working out between individual companies and countries. I think this is also your strategy.

---

[1]*George Piercy*: A senior official with Exxon who became an important negotiator with OPEC during the oil crisis. [Ed.]

Sutcliffe: We are here to discuss the whole question.

Yamani: I would like the companies to accept the principle. What is BP's position?

Sutcliffe: We want to know more about what is meant.

Yamani: This is quite simple. We want a share in the equity capital of our existing concessions. We would start with a minimum and build up to a maximum over a period of years. The exact legal form would be a matter of detail for each country. It must have the legal consequences of being a partnership.

Martin: We must know more what is involved. Can we have some more elucidation.

Yamani: We will be happy to answer questions. The minimum percentage is 20 and the maximum is 51%. Some members will ask for more than 20% initially, but the maximum is the limit for everyone.

DeCrane: Why are you unhappy with the existing arrangements?

Yamani: 1. We have the right to acquire all our natural resources but this is not our aim. We want to acquire part and stay with the companies.

2. From the legal point of view times have changed. There is a definite change in circumstances which make it necessary to readjust oil concessions. There is also a very important policy for each nation to control its own natural resources. We don't want full control but we must have some.

Martin: In spite of existing agreements?

Yamani: This is within our existing agreements. There is a principle of change of circumstances inherent in our contracts which allows this change.

DeCrane: I don't accept the doctrine, but given this, what changed circumstances have occurred to require a change in the concessions?

Yamani: The legal point is of the first importance. There is no need to go to the heart of the problem if you don't agree to changing circumstances. If you don't accept it, then let us just shake hands and say goodbye.

DeCrane: I do contest the legal theory but let us look at the fundamental problem. What is bothering you?

Yamani: Some examples of changes of circumstance are:

1. When Aramco signed its agreement, no Saudis had been to University and no Saudis had experience in the oil industry—now there are thousands of Saudi graduates and hundreds with experience in the oil industry.

2. At the date of signature, there [were] no agreements with partnership provisions. Now all new agreements provide for partnership. Even the majors are accepting it in both new and existing concessions. . . . Partnership is a must in the Middle East. Long ago we received an offer from a major for a 50% deal in Saudi Arabia. Now just recently we have another offer from a major under similar terms.

3. The trend now is to nationalize all resources. Participation is a substitute for that trend; a blend of joint venture capital and nationalization. This is our offer of partnership—a source of stability.

McQuinn: We can't accept the implication that there have been no changes since 1933. There have been many. Existing arrangements provide meaningful participation in management division of profits and access to oil. I cannot see that a change would be in the interests of longer term relationships. Why are existing arrangements unsatisfactory?

Yamani: I am very satisfied with the co-operation of the oil companies. Their people adapt to changed circumstances. There have been remarkable changes to the Aramco Agreement, all due to changes in circumstances and the companies have always been successful in readjusting to new circumstances. . . . Why aren't we satisfied? Participation is only modestly satisfying and it varies from one member to another. You don't ask a nation why it nationalizes. This is their right. We are not going as far.

Sharing of profits is not participation. It consists of a tax which is the right of Government and it also consists of royalty which is a quid for the oil in the ground. Nationals in your work force is not participation. Our right to market is a peanut. It is a substitute for royalty and does not derive from equity participation. Thus there is no participation whatsoever in our agreements today. We are not satisfied with the present but we are not planning to nationalize. We want something less.

DeCrane: If a country has exercised its sovereignty by granting concession rights, why shouldn't the party who has relied on the agreements feel that he has a right to question nationalization? You cannot ignore legal rights given by contract.

Yamani: You are exaggerating your rights. An agreement with the Government does not give immunity from nationalization and a state cannot bind its successor not to nationalize—even if they have promised not to do so. The International Court of Justice has given many decisions recognizing the right to nationalize. The U.N. resolution recognizes the right to natural resources. However we are not here to discuss nationalization.

DeCrane: I suggest we put nationalization on one side with my reservation as to the legal side. When you sign you have an agreement. Now you say this is no deal; no agreement.

Yamani: We are bound by an agreement. We can only change if circumstances change or by the exercise of our sovereign rights to nationalize with compensation. Every agreement implies the changed circumstances doctrine and there have been changed circumstances.

Hedlund: The Tehran Agreement reaffirms the original agreements. Have circumstances changed since then?

Yamani: No, the Tehran Agreement affirmed the old agreements, including the provision as to changed circumstances. There is a huge gap between the situation now and on the date of signature of these agreements. The claim of participation was prior to the Tehran Agreement.

Danner: I am worried about this implied term. You say that it is a hidden clause implicit in all agreements that if change of circumstances is in the mind of one party, then all agreements are not valid.

Yamani: It is not only in our minds but these changes of circumstances are facts. The new trend is for participation and control over natural resources. We are trying to preserve the setup and pave the way for the future and provide stability for the future. Let us see how we can both work together. We thus are sitting down not destructively but constructively to find a way to hold these agreements. You in CFP have had it happen to you the wrong way.

Danner: What is the value of an agreement with this hidden clause which enables one party to change the agreement? Where is the stability[?]

Yamani: We are reasonable and responsible. Circumstances of 30 years ago have changed. There are hundreds of cases justifying the doctrine. It is not just something in our imagination that we wish to discuss.

Kamel: The principle allowing a nation to nationalize its natural resources is well recognized and reaffirmed by the UN, OPEC Resolution 90 of 1968 established a principle of acquiring a reasonable participation. The principle of changing circumstances is well accepted. All new concessions have participation and therefore there is a new contractual standard. Oil is the most important natural resource in all OPEC countries. The companies accepted in the Tehran Agreement the application of the principle of changed circumstances. The Tehran Agreement was to implement Resolution 120 which was based on Resolution 90, therefore it is not in breach of the Tehran Agreement to ask for participation. Yesterday's agreement is a good example of a new agreement coming from changing circumstances, since in Tehran nobody had envisaged recent currency changes.

Martin: We have been reasonable.

Yamani: And should continue to be so.

DeCrane: An OPEC resolution cannot create a legal right. Changes may give rise to discussions and to changes to agreements, freely negotiated but not from any legal right. There is no legal right in our opinion to force us to agree. Therefore we must have recognized that something happened and we were practical.

Yamani: I don't care about your legal views provided you are prepared to discuss in a reasonable and practical manner. If you say there is no right to ask for participation then that is the end of the matter. If you are prepared to discuss, then we will. We have the power to move in other directions.

DeCrane: It is very important to distinguish between a right and a power.

Yamani: Good, I am glad we understand each other. For example, I own this glass and I have the right to break it. Don't make me nervous or I will use my power.

Martin: I would like to clarify our views on sovereignty over your resources. You used it to enter into agreements and you do not have the right to take the right you have granted back again. International law does not recognize such a right.

Yamani: Now I am using my right. If you get stubborn, I may use my power.

2

The Oil Crisis and the Oil Weapon

The spring of 1973 was a tumultuous time in America. What had begun in late 1972 as a few isolated revelations about questionable activities in the White House had evolved into the full-blown Watergate scandal. Although the United States had signed the Paris Peace Accords with North and South Vietnam in January 1973, government concern about the long-term stability of Southeast Asia remained intense. And six months before the Arab oil embargo began, a number of observers were declaring that an oil crisis existed.

The reason for this declaration: America was rapidly becoming reliant on imported oil. In 1973, the United States imported nearly twice as much oil as it had in 1970, and more than 15 percent of that came from the Persian Gulf region. Many factors contributed to this sudden shift, especially surging consumer demand for oil throughout the 1960s and early 1970s, at the same time that domestic production peaked, never to rise again. Although the United States still had substantial oil reserves, their volume was limited, and they would provide a smaller and smaller share of what Americans consumed.

Oil from other countries, especially Canada, Mexico, and Venezuela, would fill the gap. But what worried policymakers was the increasing share of imported oil originating from the Eastern Hemisphere. How would this change international politics? How would it affect U.S. security interests during the cold war? Could the United States regain some of its energy independence?

These questions dominated the public debate in the spring and summer of 1973. But this apparent crisis concerning oil supplies turned into a true crisis in October, when OPEC issued the first in a series of price hikes that would quadruple the price of crude oil by the new year. By October 19, Arab countries within OPEC had instituted a full embargo against the United States. With shipments of oil from the Persian Gulf halted, no end in sight of the increasing cost of petroleum products, and a cold winter settling into parts of the country, President Nixon was faced with an unprecedented energy emergency.

The documents that follow give a flavor for the variety of ways people responded to the events of 1973 and early 1974, when the embargo was lifted. Within the context of the Watergate scandal, inflation, and the recent end of U.S. involvement in the Vietnam War, the embargo and steep price hikes proved to be deeply disorienting to government leaders and ordinary Americans alike. It did indeed seem that a new world order was at hand.

5

JAMES AKINS

The Oil Crisis: This Time the Wolf Is Here
April 1973

In April 1973, the State Department's senior oil analyst, James Akins, published a piece in Foreign Affairs *that provoked a great deal of response. This article, excerpted here, not only had a provocative title but also outlined the many ways in which the United States would find itself in the hot seat if OPEC decided to exercise its political power. Akins declared that it would not be unthinkable for OPEC to use the "oil weapon"—that is, cutting back or cutting off oil supplies to countries with which it disagreed. His words proved prescient, and he went on to become ambassador to Saudi Arabia until 1975.*

That most of the world's proven oil reserves are in Arab hands is now known to the dullest observer. That the probable reserves are concentrated even more heavily in the Middle East must also be the judgment of anyone who is willing to look at the evidence. And that relations between the United States and the Arab countries are not

James Akins, "The Oil Crisis: This Time the Wolf Is Here," *Foreign Affairs*, 51 (April 1973): 462–90.

generally cordial should be clear to any newspaper reader. Even King Faisal of Saudi Arabia, who has said repeatedly that he wishes to be a friend of the United States and who believes that communism is a mortal danger to the Arabs, insists to every visitor that U.S. policy in the Middle East, which he characterizes as pro-Israeli, will ultimately drive all Arabs into the Communist camp, and that this policy will bring disaster on all America's remaining Arab friends, as earlier Anglo-American policies did to Nuri Said of Iraq.[1] Others in the Middle East frame their predictions in a different but almost equally menacing vein, in terms of a growth of radical anti-Americanism, manifesting itself in behavior that may at times be irrational.

King Faisal has also said repeatedly that the Arabs should not, and that he himself would not, allow oil to be used as a political weapon. But on this issue it seems all too likely that his is an isolated voice. In 1972, other Arabs in responsible or influential positions made no less than 15 different threats to use oil as a weapon against their "enemies." Almost all of them singled out the United States as the prime enemy.

These threats have been well publicized; the common response among Americans has been: "They need us as much as we need them"; or "They can't drink the oil"; or "Boycotts never work." But before we accept these facile responses, let us examine the facts more carefully. First of all, let us dispose of the straw man of a total cut-off of all oil supplies, which some Arab governments, at least, could not survive. Apart from threats made during the negotiations of December 1970,[2] no Arab has ever taken such a position, and Arab representatives took it at that time, in concert with other governments, for economic bargaining purposes, not for political reasons.

Rather, the usual Arab political threat is to deny oil to the Arabs' enemies, while supplies would continue to their friends. In such a case, the producing countries would still have a considerable income under almost any assumption—unless we could assume complete Western and Japanese solidarity, including a complete blocking of Arab bank accounts and an effective blocking of deliveries of essential supplies to the Arabs by the Communist countries—in other words,

---

[1] *Nuri Said* (also Nuri as-Said): Pro-British political leader and statesman in Iraq who held the position of prime minister several times between 1930 and 1958. Said was executed in a military coup that brought down the Iraqi monarchy in 1958. [Ed.]

[2] In December 1970, OPEC threatened to cut off oil supplies if its member states did not receive a minimum of 55 percent of the profits made by the companies operating within their borders. [Ed.]

something close to a war embargo. We must recognize that most of the threats are directed against Americans alone. Many of our allies and all others would be allowed to import Arab oil.

In the 1967 Six Day War a boycott was imposed against the United States on the basis of the false accusation that it had participated with Israeli planes in the attack on Cairo. The charge was quickly disproven, although the boycott lasted for over a month. It was then lifted through the efforts of Saudi Arabia, and its effects never became bothersome. We were then importing considerably less than a half-million barrels per day of oil from the Arab countries, and this was easily made up from other sources.

Today the situation would be wholly different, and tomorrow worse still. By 1980 the United States could be importing as much as eight million barrels of oil a day from the Middle East; some oil companies think it will be close to 11 million. Suppose that for some reason, political or economic, a boycott is then imposed—which, if the Middle East problem is not solved by that time, cannot be called a frivolous or unlikely hypothesis. The question we must face now, before we allow ourselves to get into such a position, is what would be our response? The choices would be difficult and limited: we could try to break the boycott through military means, i.e. war; we could accede to the wishes of the oil suppliers; or we could accept what would surely be severe damage to our economy, possibly amounting to collapse. Europe and Japan might conceivably face, or be asked by us to face, the same problems at the same time. Would their responses be in line with ours?

Moreover, a collective Arab boycott is not the only conceivable political threat. Until now the world has enjoyed the luxury of considerable surplus production capacity, relative to total demand. Now that has changed. The United States now has no spare capacity and within the next few years, assuming other producer governments and companies do not invest in huge added capacity, the production of *any one* of seven countries—Saudi Arabia, Iran, Iraq, the Federation of Arab Amirates,[3] Kuwait, Libya or Venezuela—will be larger than the combined spare capacity of the rest of the world. In other words, the loss of the production of any one of these countries could cause a temporary

---

[3]*Federation of Arab [E]mirates*: The name adopted in 1968 by a constellation of small states from what is now the United Arab Emirates, along with Bahrain and Qatar. The latter two states seceded in 1971, and the remaining states then became the United Arab Emirates. [Ed.]

but significant world oil shortage; the loss of any two could cause a crisis and quite possibly a panic among the consumers.

No, the threat to use oil as a political weapon must be taken seriously. The vulnerability of the advanced countries is too great and too plainly evident—and is about to extend to the United States. . . .

To look simply at the world's oil reserves and conclude that they are sufficient to meet the world's needs can no longer be acceptable. We could allow ourselves such fatuities as long as we had large spare oil production capacity, and while our overseas imports were small. We can do so no longer. Our security and balance-of-payments problems are large and growing. Whether we focus on today, or 1980, or 1985, it is abundantly clear that we must move on a variety of fronts if we are to avoid a situation which could lead to or even force us into highly dangerous action.

Having argued throughout this article that the oil crisis is a reality that compels urgent action, let me end on a note of hope. The current energy problem will not be a long one in human terms. By the end of the century oil will probably lose its predominance as a fuel. The measures we have the capacity to take to protect ourselves by conserving energy and developing alternative sources of energy should enable us, our allies, and the producer nations as well, to get through the next 25 years reasonably smoothly. They might even bring us smiling into the bright new world of nuclear fusion when all energy problems will be solved. This final note would ring less hollow if we did not remember the firm conviction of the late 1940s that the last fossil fuel electricity generating plant would have been built by 1970; and that in this new golden age, the home use of electricity would not even be measured. It would be so cheap, we were told, that the manpower cost of reading meters would be greater than the cost of the energy which the homeowners conceivably could consume. But perhaps in 2000 . . .

6

WILLIAM CASEY

International Ramifications
of the Energy Situation

May 1973

Some oil experts disagreed with James Akins's analysis, but most were convinced that oil stood at the center of a currently unstable international system. As Undersecretary of State for Economic Affairs William Casey said before a Senate committee in May 1973, "The international aspects of the [oil] problem are immense and pose very difficult questions in political relationships," as well as in economics. Casey's testimony, excerpted here, exemplifies how widely the "oil crisis" was understood to be both a difficult international issue and an environmental problem — an acknowledgment of humans' interdependence in using and managing the earth's natural resources that was still relatively rare outside the environmental movement.

The relationships between suppliers and consumers of energy — between oil exporters and importers—are undergoing major and rapid changes which our own increasing imports are compounding. Our emergence as the world's single most important importer of petroleum is destabilizing at this time of transition, and our importing colleagues consequently have every wish to see us take the steps necessary to limit our growth in imports. We alone among the major importing nations have a number of options open to us other than continued increases of imports. Our options are not, however, true choices. For if we do not accept them, if we simply continue to let our imports grow, we will only contribute to a further destabilization in world energy supply relationships, to greater increases in prices, and to the possibility of damaging and cutthroat competition with our friends and our allies for available energy supplies. In this context, the

William Casey, "International Ramifications of the Energy Situation," in Senate Committee on Interior and Insular Affairs, *President's Energy Message and S. 1570*, 93rd Cong., 1st Sess., May 1, 1973, 136–54.

President's recommendations for expanding the production and variety of U.S. domestic energy resources are deliberate, positive efforts to ease the impact of the entry of our burgeoning demand into the world oil market.

The members of this committee are well aware of the scope and importance of the changes taking place in international oil supply relationships. The OPEC nations are pursuing a course, in which they have been very successful in recent years, designed to increase their revenues and their control over the oil-producing concessions and much of the marketing. The international oil companies, once so dominant in assuring a steady flow of supplies and a flexibility capable of meeting emergencies, have lost much of their freedom of action and their ability to make the important decisions on price and supply. The importing governments have to face higher costs, as well as a continued tightness of supply due to the incremental rates of growth in their demand.

OPEC nations, however, also have important internal and external problems and a real interest in cooperating with consuming nations. All of these producers require the technological, economic, and political cooperation of the developed consumer nations if they are to develop lasting benefits for their future generations during this favored period in their histories. Excessive price rises could, however, create instability which would affect producers as well and bring substitute fuels into the market quicker.

In these circumstances, it is hardly surprising that the energy-importing nations have become anxious over the security and cost of their vital oil supplies. They are also keenly interested in generating the necessary exports to pay for their increasing imports and have often sought to do so by means of bilateral arrangements with the oil-exporting governments. The result has been an increasing trend toward balkanization of the oil market. While there may be advantages to individual governments pursuing their ends through bilateral agreements, and this approach may even have some appeal in the abstract, we are concerned that it can have very harmful effects in a market so heavily influenced by the decisions of a very small number of suppliers. In short, each country seems capable of obtaining its own supply security only at the expense of its neighbor's increased insecurity. The possibility of a dangerous and divisive struggle among oil-importing nations for oil supplies and export markets is real and is made more so by the degree to which we continue to increase our own imports. . . .

The principal foreign policy implication of our becoming a major importer of oil and gas is contained in the word "interdependence." Our natural resources, whether fossil fuels or ores, however immense, are finite. We must learn to use them efficiently. We must learn to conserve. But above all, we must recognize that we live on an increasingly interdependent planet and must work in harmony and cooperation with all others, regardless of political, economic, and cultural differences. This calls for even greater attention to basic programs pursued by this government, such as the reduction of trade barriers, the development of monetary stability, and above all, the generation of a generation of peace, which not only would conserve invaluable human resources but also prevent the grossest waste of the irreplaceable natural resources which have taken eons to make.

7

OLIPHANT

"... But First, Let's Hear Your Position on the Alaska Pipeline and Independent Gas Distributors!"

July 2, 1973

Americans were already concerned about an oil shortage in the summer before the embargo began. While business and government leaders argued over the causes of an emerging gas shortage, many independent refiners and gas distributors—those not owned by one of the "majors," such as Chevron or Mobil—found themselves out of supplies and charged that the majors desired such shortages to boost prices and profits. Meanwhile, the political debate about whether the government should allow drilling on the North Slope of Alaska was still swirling in Congress. In this cartoon, a vacationing motorist is held hostage by "Big Oil," presumably until he gives the "correct" responses to the political questions being posed to him.

'. . . BUT FIRST, LET'S HEAR YOUR POSITION ON THE ALASKA PIPELINE AND INDEPENDENT GAS DISTRIBUTORS!'

8

ECONOMIST

The Radical Specter of Libya

May 10, 1973

In the North African country of Libya, a bloodless coup in 1969 brought down the monarchy and eventually put into power a young military officer named Muammar al-Qaddafi. Throughout the 1960s, Qaddafi had been a fervent supporter of Gamal Abdel Nasser's Arab nationalist ideals (as had Saddam Hussein in Iraq) and believed that Arab countries within the Middle East should become more politically unified to counter the international power of the United States and other Western countries. Like Nasser and other Pan-Arabists, he brought to these ideas socialist leanings that would lead him to nationalize a number of businesses in Libya, most notably the foreign oil companies. Although Iraq had nation-

"Qaddafi's Bid," *Economist*, May 10, 1973, 111.

alized its oil industry in 1972, Libya's consideration of that move in the spring of 1973, followed by its actual nationalization of oil operations in September, attracted much more attention within the context of growing anxiety about worldwide oil supplies. In the following article, the Economist *(a British weekly magazine) saw the nationalization of the Libyan oil industry as a threat to foreign oil companies across the Middle East.*

A charismatic, self-identified revolutionary, Qaddafi was also accused of financing terrorist groups in the Middle East and attacks on westerners and Israelis. Throughout the 1970s and 1980s, the U.S. government reviled Qaddafi and considered him one of the most dangerous foreign leaders. Since the 1990s, however, Qaddafi has moderated and has opened his country up to foreign energy companies eager to develop Libya's remaining oil reserves and rich natural gas fields.

The oil companies have always expected that negotiations with Libya over the government's participation in the industry would be difficult. Early this week the government dropped what was a bombshell even to them. It demanded 100 percent participation in the six American companies operating in the country. Does this mean the total nationalization inflicted on British Petroleum by Colonel Qaddafi, or is it merely a negotiating position? That question kept the companies on tenterhooks until their meeting with the Libyans originally scheduled for Thursday.

Taken at face value, the demand looks impossible to meet. It would give Libya considerably more than Saudi Arabia, Kuwait, Qatar and Abu Dhabi have settled for, or the equivalent deal Iran has accepted. It would undermine all the progress laboriously made so far. There might be some chance of persuading these countries to stick to their agreements, no matter what happens in Libya, but it is a chance that the oil companies would prefer not to take—especially as the Kuwaiti parliament has yet to ratify the agreement and details are still being worked out with the Iranians.

Libya's demands, emphasized on Tuesday by a token 24-hour stoppage of oil exports from its terminals, call for a 100 percent control of company facilities, with compensation based only on the net book value of their assets. By 100 percent control, the Libyans could be aiming for the kind of deal negotiated by Iran, which simply scattered a number of nationals through the management at board level but left the operating companies virtually intact. If this is what Libya means, the demand is negotiable. But that is unlikely. If it wants 100 percent of the equity, there will be trouble. The broad participation agreements negotiated so far give a mere 25 percent share of the equity to the Arab producers. This will rise to only 51 percent by 1983. . . .

If negotiations with Libya break down, the consequences could be serious. Should Libya cut off its oil, Europe and America would share out available supplies. But if the cut were to last much more than a month, both Europe and America would probably have to start thinking about rationing petrol [gasoline] and other oil products. Libya meanwhile could live on its accumulated gold and currency reserves. While no one knows for sure how much cash is in the Libyan reserves, it is thought to be sufficient for a year.

9

NATIONAL REVIEW

Confronting Libya
September 28, 1973

Qaddafi's mix of Pan-Arabist tendencies and socialist ideals did not sit well with most Americans, least of all conservatives. In response to Libya's nationalizing of its oil industry, the conservative magazine National Review *published the following editorial just weeks before the Arab oil embargo. The kind of aggressive rhetoric seen here would reappear in the spring of 1975 with Miles Ignotus's article "Seizing Arab Oil" (Document 26).*

Even as Qaddafi was nationalizing all foreign oil companies in Libya, Saudi Arabia's King Faisal, hitherto the U.S.'s staunchest and most powerful friend in the Arab world, made it known that he will use his country's immense oil reserves as a negotiating weapon against the U.S. until he sees a change in the "one-sided" American policy of "favoritism to Zionism and support against the Arabs." President Nixon's response to all this was twofold: (1) He issued, at a news con-

"Turning On (Off) the Heat," *National Review*, September 28, 1973, 1042.

ference, some of his most even-handed remarks to date about the Mideast impasse, blaming "both sides"; (2) he warned that the U.S. will make every effort to reduce its dependency on Arab oil.

It was of course the second of these responses that the *New York Times* endorsed at considerable editorial length. In the back, somewhere, of Arab as well as Western minds—and perhaps serving as an unexpressed counter in the bargaining—there remains a third course of action which few people mention, let alone demand: seizing, say, Libya. Not to *appropriate* the oil, but to guarantee its availability at the world market price. . . . The doctrines of national self-determination and territorial integrity—according to which a Qaddafi is entirely justified in his actions—may seem worse than vapid on the wintry day when Americans—or Europeans or Japanese—are shuddering in heatless homes, stranded there with gasless cars. Such doctrines will then seem a flimsy pretext for an upstart despot's repudiation of his country's obligations. Indeed, a new variant of an old liberal question may then come into play: Why should a tiny fraction of the world's population be allowed to sit capriciously on such a desperately needed resource? And then the heat *will* be on.

10

RANAN R. LURIE

"The Arab Oil Barons Set the Pace"

September 17, 1973

In this cartoon, President Richard Nixon is flanked on either side by Muammar al-Qaddafi, the head of Libya, and King Faisal of Saudi Arabia. Libya was initially the most aggressive of the OPEC countries to punish the United States for its support of Israel. Although Faisal's family had long-established ties to American oil companies and the U.S. government, Saudi Arabia remained the most important player in OPEC because of its huge oil reserves.

Ranan R. Lurie, "The Arab Oil Barons Set the Pace: For Mr. Nixon and America, There Were Only Painful Choices," *Newsweek*, September 17, 1973, 33.

The Arab oil barons set the pace: For Mr. Nixon and America, there were only painful choices

11

ARAMCO EXECUTIVES

Memorandum to President Nixon

October 12, 1973

Despite months of concerns about an oil supply crisis, the country was nonetheless shocked when a true crisis began to take shape. On October 6, 1973, Egyptian and Syrian forces launched a surprise attack against Israel in hopes of regaining territory they had lost in the Six-Day War (1967). The Soviet Union sent arms to Egypt and Syria. The United States responded in kind by providing military support to Israel. On October 12, the chairmen of the four major oil companies in Saudi Arabia, which had joined together in 1948 to form a joint company called Aramco, wrote a memo to President Nixon, urging him to take seriously the fact that U.S. oil interests in the region were now under threat.

"Memorandum to the President," Oil Box 2, Folder 10, John J. McCloy Papers, Amherst College Library, Amherst, Mass.

1. The oil industry in the Free World is now operating "wide open," with essentially no spare capacity.

2. The terms demanded by OPEC at Vienna[1] are of such a magnitude that their impact could produce a serious disruption in the balance of payments position of the Western world.

3. The demands, if acceded to or imposed, could increase the Free World oil cost from the Persian Gulf alone by $15 billion per year.

4. Market forces have pushed crude prices up substantially. A significant increase in posted prices and in the revenues of the producing countries appear justified under these circumstances; but the magnitude of the increase demanded by OPEC, which is in the order of a 100 percent increase, is unacceptable. Any increase should be one which allows the parties an opportunity to adjust to the situation in an orderly fashion. Accordingly, the companies are resisting the OPEC demands and they are seeking an adjustment of them which can be fair to all the parties concerned.

5. In the midst of pressing these demands vigorously, the Arab negotiators in Vienna have stated that their governments were angered by the speech of Ambassador Scali[2] before the United Nations which they interpreted as a clear expression of support of the Israeli position by reason of its specification of the October 6 boundaries. They also report that a request from the United States to King Faisal that he urge Arab combatants to retire to this ceasefire line produced great irritation. We have been told that the Saudis will impose some cut-back in crude oil production as a result of the United States position taken thus far. A further and much more substantial move will be taken by Saudi Arabia and Kuwait in the event of further evidence of increased U.S. support of the Israeli position.

6. We are convinced of the seriousness of the intentions of the Saudis and Kuwaitis and that any actions of the U.S. government at this time in terms of increased military aid to Israel will have a critical and adverse effect on our relations with the moderate Arab producing countries.

7. In the present highly charged climate in the Middle East, there is a high probability that a single action taken by one producer government against the United States would have a snowballing effect that would produce a major petroleum supply crisis.

---

[1] OPEC moved its headquarters from Geneva, Switzerland, to Vienna, Austria, in 1965. Tense negotiations between OPEC ministers and the oil companies began on October 8 and were broken off October 12. [Ed.]

[2] *John A. Scali*: appointed U.S. ambassador to the United Nations in 1973. [Ed.]

8. The bulk of the oil produced in the Persian Gulf goes to Japan and Western Europe. These countries cannot face a serious shut-in. Regardless of what happens to United States interests in the Middle East, we believe they will of necessity continue to seek Middle East oil and that they may be forced to expand their Middle East supply positions at our expense.

9. Much more than our commercial interests in the area is now at hazard. The whole position of the United States in the Middle East is on the way to being seriously impaired, with Japanese, European, and perhaps Russian interests largely supplanting United States presence in the area, to the detriment of both our economy and our security.

J. K. JAMIESON
Chairman, Exxon Corporation

RAWLEIGH WARNER, JR.
Chairman, Mobil Oil Corporation

M. F. GRANVILLE
Chairman, Texaco, Inc.

OTTO N. MILLER, Chairman
Standard Oil Company of California

12

TIME

Unsheathing the Political Weapon

October 29, 1973

During the first few weeks of the oil crisis, a number of things were unclear. Were the Arab countries of OPEC going to institute an all-out embargo or simply reduce their output? How high would OPEC go in setting the price of its oil? Could oil from other countries satisfy American demand? One certainty emerged immediately, however: Americans were going to have to take stock of how much oil and gasoline they used, with an eye toward scaling back their consumption.

"Unsheathing the Political Weapon," *Time*, October 29, 1973, 50–51.

After long muttering vaguely about using their abundant oil as a "political weapon," the newly unified Arab leaders finally unsheathed it last week. They vowed to cut the oil production on which the fuel-short West depends and to raise prices sharply. That oil squeeze could easily lead to cold homes, hospitals and schools, shuttered factories, slower travel, brownouts, consumer rationing, aggravated inflation and even worsened air pollution in the U.S., Europe and Japan.

The Arabs took three steps:

1. Ten Arab countries meeting in Kuwait decided that each month from now on they will reduce oil output at least 5% below the preceding month. The cutbacks will continue, they said, "until an Israeli withdrawal is completed, and until the restoration of the legal rights of the Palestinian people."

2. King F[a]isal of Saudi Arabia, the biggest Mideast producer, at first decreed a 10% cut in output. But by week's end, as the war seemed to be going against the Arabs, he announced a total ban on oil shipments to the U.S. Presently, 3.4% of the crude oil consumed daily by the U.S. comes from Saudi Arabia. Libya, Algeria and Abu Dhabi also announced embargos.

3. Six Persian Gulf oil countries lifted the posted price of crude oil (a theoretical figure on which royalties and taxes are based) by a stunning 70%, to $5.11 per [barrel (bbl.)]. It will keep Arab oil revenues rising—helping to pay for the war against Israel—even as fewer barrels are shipped out. It will also force Americans, Europeans and Japanese to pay as much as 5¢ per gal. more for gasoline, heating oil and other products.

Parts of the Arab oil strategy are still unclear. The communiqué from Kuwait, for instance, left deliberately vague the political conditions under which the 5%-a-month production cuts would be restored; it made no attempt to define "Palestinian rights." Further, the Arabs promised to slash shipments only to "unfriendly" countries. That pledge is impossible to carry out because the Arabs have little control over where oil goes once it leaves their ports.

Some Western diplomats and oilmen thought that the production cuts were about the most modest that the Arabs could have agreed on. In fact, before settling on the 5%-a-month formula, the Kuwait conference rejected proposals for a three-month total shutoff of oil exports and for an immediate 50% reduction in production.

None of that is really reassuring, though; the Arabs essentially have the West over a 42-gal. oil barrel. World oil use will more than double during the 1970s. Slaking that intense thirst requires continual swift increases in output, and there is only one place they can come from. The desert sands of the Arab nations hold at least 300 billion bbl. of easily recoverable oil, or 60% of the proven reserves in the non-Communist world. Merely by increasing production more slowly than the West desires—let alone reducing it—the Arabs could cause considerable discomfort.

The severity of the blow will vary widely from region to region:

The U.S. superficially would seem well able to withstand a sellers' boycott. The nation now imports about a third of the 17 million bbl. of oil it burns each day, but no more than 11% comes from the Arab countries. Cutbacks could prompt other major suppliers to reduce sales to the U.S. in order to conserve supplies in a tight global market. Even so, an eventual 25% slice in Arab output would cut U.S. supply about 2,000,000 bbl. a day.

Unfortunately, those barrels are critical. The U.S. is running short of oil and needs every drop it can get. Airlines are discussing scheduling fewer flights. Democratic Senator Henry Jackson of Washington has introduced a bill that would, among other things, lower the speed limits on interstate highways to 50 mph or less and force some utilities to convert from oil to higher-polluting coal. The most chilling aspect of an oil embargo—literally—is that the U.S. might be unable to stay warm this winter. The Interior Department figures that the nation will have to import 650,000 bbl. of heating oil a day to supply adequate heat, but Economist Lawrence Goldstein of the Petroleum Industry Research Foundation fears that other countries will sell only 350,000 bbl. a day. White House Aide Melvin Laird offers this advice: "I'd buy a sweater."

Western Europe imports 72% of its oil from the Arab countries, and it has even fewer alternative sources than the U.S. Price increases could add $1 billion to Britain's trade deficit next year. Supply shortages will take longer to show up—about a month's supply of Arab oil is headed for European ports in tankers already at sea—but eventually shortages are a real threat. Giovanni Theodoli, president of Chevron Oil Italiana, fears a 20% drop in Italian crude-oil imports over the next six months, and worries that "we are not going to have enough energy to support our industry." The British government already has printed ration books and stacked them in post offices.

Japan has to import almost all of its oil, 82% from the Mideast. Surprisingly, the Japanese are fairly calm largely because they believe that they can negotiate special deals with the Arabs. Perhaps they can, but the deals would be swung at the expense of U.S. and European supplies, and of higher prices for the Japanese consumer.

All this assumes that the Arabs actually carry out their threats. Before last week's moves, U.S. Energy Expert Robert Hunter expressed skepticism that an Arab oil cutback would work, even as part of a war against Israel, because "every oil producer would be watching every other one to see which was trying to carve out a larger place in long-term markets by violating a proclaimed embargo."

In the Arab nations the West is facing something new: a group of countries that do not need the money that they could get by expanding output. By 1980 the Arab countries will be getting at least $50 billion a year for their oil. The Arabs believe, with some justice, that the price of oil can go only one way—up. Oil kept in the ground is thus a kind of savings account. It will be worth more in, say, 1976 than it is today.

What can the West do to counter the Arab oil weapon? There has been some talk of freezing the billions of dollars of Arab accounts in Western banks. [Massachusetts Institute of Technology] Professor Morris Adelman, a leading oil expert, goes so far as to advocate a threat of military occupation of some Arab oil fields. Much more constructively, the West could form a consumers' cooperative that would allocate supplies among nations. The U.S. has made some attempts in this direction, but they have not got far. There is, in fact, a strong danger that the exact opposite will happen: consuming countries would bid against each other for available Arab oil, starting a kind of worldwide auction.

Oil consumers could also greatly accelerate research into ways of efficiently developing non-Arab sources of fuel. The Rocky Mountain shale and Athabascan tar sands of Canada may hold more oil than all the sands of the Arab deserts; some estimates run as high as 1.5 trillion bbl. Liquefication and gasification of coal could provide a low-polluting way of using that superabundant fuel. But the capital investment required is staggering: $5 billion to $7 billion to get 1,000,000 bbl. of oil a day out of shale or tar sands. Senator Jackson has been advocating a U.S. emergency research effort similar to the Manhattan Project that produced the atomic bomb. James Akins, the newly appointed U.S. Ambassador to Saudi Arabia, goes further to suggest a supranational authority that would coordinate research among all the oil-consuming countries.

Both ideas are sound. Indeed, by prompting the consuming nations to investigate seriously new sources of energy, and to rethink their profligate energy-using habits, the Arabs could eventually do the West a favor. But that is for the very long run; meanwhile, the U.S. and other oil-consuming countries had best prepare for a real squeeze.

13

RICHARD NIXON

The Energy Emergency

November 7, 1973

It did not take long for the president to appear on television and inform the American people about the government's plan to handle the crisis. Nixon did not sugarcoat the situation, noting that the country was "heading toward the most acute shortages of energy since World War II," when oil was rationed. Emphasizing the short-term need for conservation, he also laid out long-term plans that he incorporated under the slogan "Project Independence." An excerpt from his speech is included here.

Good evening.

I want to talk to you tonight about a serious national problem, a problem we must all face together in the months and years ahead.

As America has grown and prospered in recent years, our energy demands have begun to exceed available supplies. In recent months, we have taken many actions to increase supplies and to reduce consumption. But even with our best efforts, we knew that a period of temporary shortages was inevitable.

Unfortunately, our expectations for this winter have now been sharply altered by the recent conflict in the Middle East. Because of that war, most of the Middle Eastern oil producers have reduced overall production and cut off their shipments of oil to the United States. By the end of this month, more than 2 million barrels a day of oil we expected to import into the United States will no longer be available.

Richard Nixon, "The Energy Emergency," in http://www.presidency.ucsb.edu/ws/index.php?pid=4034&st=&st1=.

We must, therefore, face up to a very stark fact: We are heading toward the most acute shortages of energy since World War II. Our supply of petroleum this winter will be at least 10 percent short of our anticipated demands, and it could fall short by as much as 17 percent.

Now, even before war broke out in the Middle East, these prospective shortages were the subject of intensive discussions among members of my Administration, leaders of the Congress, Governors, mayors, and other groups. From these discussions has emerged a broad agreement that we, as a Nation, must now set upon a new course.

In the short run, this course means that we must use less energy—that means less heat, less electricity, less gasoline. In the long run, it means that we must develop new sources of energy which will give us the capacity to meet our needs without relying on any foreign nation.

The immediate shortage will affect the lives of each and every one of us. In our factories, our cars, our homes, our offices, we will have to use less fuel than we are accustomed to using. Some school and factory schedules may be realigned, and some jet airplane flights will be canceled.

This does not mean that we are going to run out of gasoline or that air travel will stop or that we will freeze in our homes or offices anyplace in America. The fuel crisis need not mean genuine suffering for any American. But it will require some sacrifice by all Americans.

We must be sure that our most vital needs are met first—and that our least important activities are the first to be cut back. And we must be sure that while the fat from our economy is being trimmed, the muscle is not seriously damaged.

To help us carry out that responsibility, I am tonight announcing the following steps:

First, I am directing that industries and utilities which use coal—which is our most abundant resource—be prevented from converting from coal to oil. Efforts will also be made to convert power plants from the use of oil to the use of coal.

Second, we are allocating reduced quantities of fuel for aircraft. Now, this is going to lead to a cutback of more than 10 percent of the number of flights and some rescheduling of arrival and departure times.

Third, there will be reductions of approximately 15 percent in the supply of heating oil for homes and offices and other establishments. To be sure that there is enough oil to go around for the entire winter, all over the country, it will be essential for all of us to live and work in lower temperatures. We must ask everyone to lower the thermostat in your home by at least 6 degrees, so that we can achieve a national day-time average of 68 degrees. Incidentally, my doctor tells me that in a temperature of 66 to 68 degrees, you are really more healthy than when it is 75 to 78, if that is any comfort. In offices, factories, and commercial establishments, we must ask that you achieve the equivalent of a 10-degree reduction by either lowering the thermostat or curtailing working hours.

Fourth, I am ordering additional reductions in the consumption of energy by the Federal Government. We have already taken steps to reduce the Government's consumption by 7 percent. The cuts must now go deeper and must be made by every agency and every department in the Government. I am directing that the daytime temperatures in Federal offices be reduced immediately to a level of between 65 and 68 degrees, and that means in this room, too, as well as in every other room in the White House. In addition, I am ordering that all vehicles owned by the Federal Government—and there are over a half-million of them—travel no faster than 50 miles per hour except in emergencies. This is a step which I have also asked Governors, mayors, and local officials to take immediately with regard to vehicles under their authority.

Fifth, I am asking the Atomic Energy Commission to speed up the licensing and construction of nuclear plants. We must seek to reduce the time required to bring nuclear plants on line—nuclear plants that can produce power—to bring them on line from 10 years to 6 years, reduce that time lag.

Sixth, I am asking that Governors and mayors reinforce these actions by taking appropriate steps at the State and local level. We have already learned, for example, from the State of Oregon, that considerable amounts of energy can be saved simply by curbing unnecessary lighting and slightly altering the school year. I am recommending that other communities follow this example and also seek ways to stagger working hours, to encourage greater use of mass transit and car pooling.

How many times have you gone along the highway or the freeway, wherever the case may be, and see hundreds and hundreds of cars with only one individual in that car. This we must all cooperate to change.

Consistent with safety and economic considerations, I am also asking Governors to take steps to reduce highway speed limits to 50 miles per hour. This action alone, if it is adopted on a nationwide basis, could save over 200,000 barrels of oil a day—just reducing the speed limit to 50 miles per hour.

Now, all of these actions will result in substantial savings of energy. More than that, most of these are actions that we can take right now—without further delay.

The key to their success lies, however, not just here in Washington, but in every home, in every community across this country. If each of us joins in this effort, joins with the spirit and the determination that have always graced the American character, then half the battle will already be won.

But we should recognize that even these steps, as essential as they are, may not be enough. We must be prepared to take additional steps, and for that purpose, additional authorities must be provided by the Congress. . . .

It is only prudent that we be ready to cut the consumption of oil products, such as gasoline, by rationing, or by a fair system of taxation, and consequently, I have directed that contingency plans, if this becomes necessary, be prepared for that purpose.

Now, some of you may wonder whether we are turning back the clock to another age. Gas rationing, oil shortages, reduced speed limits—they all sound like a way of life we left behind with Glenn Miller[1] and the war of the forties. Well, in fact, part of our current problem also stems from war—the war in the Middle East. But our deeper energy problems come not from war, but from peace and from abundance. We are running out of energy today because our economy has grown enormously and because in prosperity what were once considered luxuries are now considered necessities.

How many of you can remember when it was very unusual to have a home air-conditioned? And yet, this is very common in almost all parts of the Nation.

As a result, the average American will consume as much energy in the next 7 days as most other people in the world will consume in an entire year. We have only 6 percent of the world's people in America, but we consume over 30 percent of all the energy in the world.

Now, our growing demands have bumped up against the limits of available supply, and until we provide new sources of energy for tomorrow, we must be prepared to tighten our belts today.

Let me turn now to our long-range plans.

While a resolution of the immediate crisis is our highest priority, we must also act now to prevent a recurrence of such a crisis in the

---

[1] *Glenn Miller:* Popular bandleader in the late 1930s and early 1940s. [Ed.]

future. This is a matter of bipartisan concern. It is going to require a bipartisan response.

Two years ago, in the first energy message any President has ever sent to the Congress, I called attention to our urgent energy problem. Last April, this year, I reaffirmed to the Congress the magnitude of that problem, and I called for action on seven major legislative initiatives. Again in June, I called for action. I have done so frequently since then.

But thus far, not one major energy bill that I have asked for has been enacted. I realize that the Congress has been distracted in this period by other matters. But the time has now come for the Congress to get on with this urgent business—providing the legislation that will meet not only the current crisis but also the long-range challenge that we face. . . .

We must have the legislation now which will authorize construction of the Alaska pipeline—legislation which is not burdened with irrelevant and unnecessary provisions.

We must have legislative authority to encourage production of our vast quantities of natural gas, one of the cleanest and best sources of energy.

We must have the legal ability to set reasonable standards for the surface mining of coal.

And we must have the organizational structures to meet and administer our energy programs. . . .

Finally, I have stressed repeatedly the necessity of increasing our energy research and development efforts. Last June, I announced a 5-year, $10 billion program to develop better ways of using energy and to explore and develop new energy sources. Last month I announced plans for an immediate acceleration of that program.

We can take heart from the fact that we in the United States have half the world's known coal reserves. We have huge, untapped sources of natural gas. We have the most advanced nuclear technology known to man. We have oil in our continental shelves. We have oil shale out in the Western part of the United States, and we have some of the finest technical and scientific minds in the world. In short, we have all the resources we need to meet the great challenge before us. Now we must demonstrate the will to meet that challenge. . . .

Let us unite in committing the resources of this Nation to a major new endeavor, an endeavor that in this Bicentennial Era we can appropriately call "Project Independence."

Let us set as our national goal, in the spirit of Apollo, with the determination of the Manhattan Project, that by the end of this decade we will have developed the potential to meet our own energy needs without depending on any foreign energy sources.

Let us pledge that by 1980, under Project Independence, we shall be able to meet America's energy needs from America's own energy resources. . . .

We have an energy crisis, but there is no crisis of the American spirit. Let us go forward, then, doing what needs to be done, proud of what we have accomplished together in the past, and confident of what we can accomplish together in the future.

Let us find in this time of national necessity a renewed awareness of our capacities as a people, a deeper sense of our responsibilities as a Nation, and an increased understanding that the measure and the meaning of America has always been determined by the devotion which each of us brings to our duty as citizens of America.

14

ROBERT ZSCHIESCHE

"I Want You to Lower Your Thermostat"

December 3, 1973

Uncle Sam has played a prominent role in America's visual culture since the early nineteenth century. Although the character was invented during the War of 1812, it was not until the late 1830s that political cartoonist Thomas Nast began drawing the figure we recognize as Uncle Sam today. The cartoon reprinted here, caricaturing President Nixon, plays off the World War I recruiting poster that shows a very stern Uncle Sam pointing a finger at the reader and saying, "I Want YOU for U.S. Army." Robert Zschiesche was not the only editorial cartoonist who used Uncle Sam to portray the nation at crisis during 1973–1974. In fact, Uncle Sam made frequent appearances in editorial cartoons about the oil embargo, often standing in stark contrast to caricatures of Arab "oil sheikhs."

Robert Zschiesche, "I Want You to Lower Your Thermostat," *Time*, December 3, 1973, 29.

15

Experiencing the Oil Squeeze
November–December 1973

The oil crisis dominated news reports in the fall of 1973, and by far the topic addressed most often was conservation. Such discussions helped Americans imagine what steps they and their government could take to control the situation. But taking such steps required a radical rethinking among Americans, who had long been accustomed to cheap gas.

Mideast Oil Stops Flowing—and U.S. Feels First Pinch

November 19, 1973

In this document, U.S. News and World Report *detailed the myriad ways that individuals and government responded to President Nixon's speech on the "energy emergency."*

Even as President Nixon was proclaiming an "energy emergency" on nationwide radio and television, Americans were taking steps to meet the crisis.

In Columbia, S.C., official city cars now are limited to a speed of no more than 50 mph, and thermostats in city buildings are turned down to 68 degrees. A fleet of seven bicycles is on hand for employee use in the downtown business district.

Speed limits on the Pennsylvania Turnpike and New Jersey's three major expressways have been cut to 50 mph, instead of 60 to 70 mph.

For students in schools of Carroll County, Ga., there will be no more band or field trips on school buses.

The Chamber of Commerce in Greenwich, Conn., reports Christmas lighting along two of the city's major streets probably will be curtailed.

The 500 residents of Block Island, R.I., have gone back to daylight-saving time so electric lights will not be used so much in the evening. The town council has even discussed the possibility of using windmills to generate electricity.

State buildings in Ohio are being kept at 68 degrees in daytime, 65 at night and 60 on weekends. Lighting will be reduced to the absolute minimum. Incentives are to be given to employees who come to work in car pools of three or more persons.

Radio station KFWB in Los Angeles is signing up listeners for car pools. Computers will be used to match them up by geographical areas.

Los Angeles County officials expect to adopt an ordinance providing authority to reduce or eliminate electrically lighted advertising.

"Mideast Oil Stops Flowing—and U.S. Feels First Pinch," *U.S. News and World Report,* November 19, 1973, 29.

The Southern California Rapid Transit District, facing a shortage of diesel fuel, may have to cut back daily schedules and do away with all Sunday bus service.

Bank of America will have no "tree of lights" at its world headquarters in San Francisco this year, and most holiday lighting in cities along the California coast will be restricted.

Governor Tom McCall of Oregon is warning that those who violate his order against outdoor display lighting will lose all electric service. This is just one of the many stringent measures that are being taken in Pacific Northwest States already hard hit by a power shortage because a drought reduced the water supply needed to operate hydroelectric turbines.

Such measures have cut electricity use in the Northwest by 7 to 8 percent, proving it can be done. Some examples—

Many offices find light is adequate with two of the four bulbs in fluorescent lighting units removed. A bank's air conditioning keeps things comfortable operating 13 hours a day, rather than 20 as previously. A factory reduced lighting in its parking lot by 65 percent. In Seattle, 626 lighted billboards have not been turned on since November 1.

Washington State Governor Daniel Evans may offer free use of toll bridges to cars carrying four or more riders. He already has joined the Governors of Georgia, South Carolina, New Jersey and other States in setting a speed limit of 50 mph for official cars.

In Illinois, the limit for State autos has been put at 55 mph. Governor Daniel Walker has ordered that any new cars purchased for State use must be subcompact models.

Robert Samuels, president of Yellow Cab Company in Chicago, has told drivers to aim for a fuel cut of 10 percent by driving slower, turning off motors when parked and avoiding aimless cruising.

The Federal Government itself is under orders to reduce energy use by at least 7 percent throughout its far-flung activities.

The Department of Defense, which uses about 2.4 percent of all U.S. fuel consumed, claims to have achieved a 14 percent reduction since last May. The Navy's ships now cruise at 16 knots an hour instead of the 20 that had been normal. Air Force pilots are training more in flight simulators instead of planes.

Traditionally drafty barracks are chillier than ever—many at temperatures below the recommended 68 degrees. At the Pentagon, long corridors are dimly lit because most light bulbs have been unscrewed. About 250 parking spaces have been set aside for car poolers.

And at the White House, Nixon aides don sweaters against the chill of 68-degree temperatures, electric-driven fountains are turned off, and outside lights are cut off at 10 P.M.

Elsewhere across the nation, lights are out on many well-known structures, including the prominent Wrigley Building in Chicago, which has been lighted almost continually for nearly 50 years.

TIME

The New Highway Guerrillas

December 17, 1973

In this article, Time *detailed why truckers were among those Americans hit hardest—and earliest—by fuel shortages.*

When times are flush, the life of a trucker can be good—not easy, but good. Highballing down a turnpike in his own $30,000 rig, the open countryside flashing by, the air conditioning and stereo on, old buddies to meet at the next truck stop, a good load in back and the promise of maybe $20,000 in profit at the end of the year—a man could do worse. But times now are anything but flush, and the truckers have suddenly turned into the angriest and most disruptive group of protesters in the nation.

What could cause the truckers, normally strong law-and-order men, to become a bunch of traffic-blocking guerrillas? The highway tie-ups that they organized last week were called to vent these gripes:

— Lower speed limits: Truckers claim that their rigs run more efficiently at 65 mph than at the 55-mph limit already in effect in many states and slated to become the national standard. On the contrary, a General Motors computer study indicates that trucks burn 15% less fuel going 50 to 55 mph than when doing 70. The real issue in the cabs is not fuel economy but money in the wallet. Most hired drivers are paid by the mile, not the hour; the 400,000 who pilot their own rigs must try to haul as many loads as possible in a week. Averaging 55 rather than

"The New Highway Guerrillas," *Time*, December 17, 1973, 33.

70, they can cover 150 fewer miles in a ten-hour driving day; at 16¢ a mile, that translates to $24 less every working day for a hired driver and, at 40¢ a mile, $60 less each day for an owner-operator.

— Fuel prices: Until three months ago, diesel fuel averaged around 27¢ per gal. Now it costs 45¢ to 51¢ and has gone as high as 80¢ at the pumps of at least one Ohio truck stop. Typically, a trucker grosses $300 hauling a load between Pittsburgh and Chicago and keeps $55 as profit. Rocketing fuel prices now slash that profit by $23. The truckers want the government to set a diesel-fuel ceiling of 35.9¢ per gal. Transportation Secretary Claude Brinegar and the Cost of Living Council have agreed to look into charges of price gouging by truck stops.

— Fuel scarcity: When truckers say "Fill 'er up," they are calling for 100 or more gallons; typically, their tanks hold 120 to 140 gal. Now many stations are limiting them to 50, 25 or even 10 gal. at a time. So the drivers must chase from truck stop to truck stop, wasting precious driving time, to keep their four-miles-to-the-gallon rigs running. The drivers want a generous allocation of fuel to the truck stops to keep them on the road.

These problems are no excuse for continuing illegal highway blockades. "Holding the public hostage because there is a fuel shortage would be totally irresponsible and counterproductive," says Thomas C. Schumacher Jr., managing director of the California Trucking Association. Such talk does not impress the truckers. One driver, sitting in the cab of a tractor-trailer that was blocking traffic approaching the Delaware Memorial Bridge last week, said: "We want Nixon and his people, when they turn on their television sets, to hear us."

16

Citizens Respond to the Oil Crisis
January 1974

*The Arab oil embargo and OPEC's price hikes hit family budgets extraor-
dinarily hard. The most immediate and visible sign came at the gas
pump, of course, but the rapidly increasing transportation costs meant
that inflation spiraled through the economy. In the Northeast, which
relied predominantly on oil to heat homes, working-class and middle-
class families had to absorb skyrocketing oil prices during the winter on
top of the other inflationary pressures. People expressed their anger and
frustration in many ways, including editorials and letters to the editor.
The following documents are from the* Berkshire Eagle, *a newspaper
published in the small industrial city of Pittsfield, Massachusetts.*

BERKSHIRE EAGLE
Is the Crisis for Real?
January 3, 1974

The Berkshire Eagle's *lead editorial for January 3, 1974, represented a
common reaction among American citizens: irritation with the U.S. government and major oil companies for not adequately explaining the
causes of the crisis. The editorial notes that even the head of the newly
established Federal Energy Administration, William E. Simon, seemed
uncertain about "the dimensions of the crisis." Having made his name
on Wall Street, Simon had no previous experience with the oil business
or energy markets, and by the summer of 1974, he had moved on to
become Nixon's (and later Ford's) treasury secretary.*

By common consent, energy boss Will E. Simon seems to have been
labeled one of the Good Guys in an administration that has all too few

"Is the Crisis for Real?" (editorial), *Berkshire Eagle*, January 3, 1974, p. 18.

of them. The reporters and the politicians like him. He's open and candid; he meets the press frequently; he talks plain English.

But Mr. Simon also seems to be laboring under the same handicap as just about everyone else in and out of the government. He doesn't really know the dimensions of the crisis he has been asked to save us from.

This was nicely illustrated at his press conference last week when he was asked how he would decide when and if the time to impose gas rationing on the American public has arrived.

"Well," said Mr. Simon, "I would say a critical factor would be if people begin queuing up at gas stations for three and four hours at a time. I don't think we can tolerate that."

Indeed we can't. But those two sentences say volumes about the fuzziness of our comprehension of the fuel shortage, even at the top level. As Washington correspondent Martin F. Nolan of the *Boston Globe* commented: "A government policy based solely on visible chaos is something to ponder."

One reason the policy has to be based on visible chaos is that the government simply doesn't have the facts and figures necessary for approaching the problem in a more orderly fashion. What data it does have on oil supplies comes from the oil industry. And as the *New York Times* observed the other day, "the world petroleum market has traditionally operated under shrouds of such murkiness that the business of arms smuggling seems like an open bazaar by comparison."

Hence the wildly disparate figures emanating from various official sources on the very basic question of just how big the gap between demand and supply is at present, let alone what it may be a month or two from now. Hence, also, the increasing befuddlement and cynicism among plain citizens who are being told to turn down thermostats and grab up all the firewood they can at the same time they are reading about tankers stacked up 20 deep outside U.S. ports because the fuel tanks are overloaded and there is no place to deposit their cargoes.

The result of all this is that the average American quite obviously is not persuaded that the "crisis" is for real. The widespread supposition that the whole thing is a giant conspiracy by the big oil producers to push up prices and force out independent competition is no doubt a gross oversimplification, nurtured in part by the fact that the Nixon scandals have made us all overly susceptible to conspiracy theories. But certainly the inability of government to define the problem in specific terms has done nothing to allay these dark suspicions.

Thus far, the public has tolerated the official confusion with surprisingly good grace. For one thing, whether the immediate crisis is for real or not, no one can argue with the desirability of cutting down on our prodigal misuse of finite energy resources. For another thing, the effects at this point are in the nature of slight public inconvenience rather than serious hardship.

But if and when the effects become more severe, if fuel prices go out of sight and plant closings become common, the public tolerance is likely to shift to high indignation. And the oil companies that have been riding so high are likely to find themselves confronted with a demand for close governmental regulation so overwhelming that even their friends in the White House will be unable to keep it from coming to pass.

BERKSHIRE EAGLE

Is Oil a Public Utility?

January 11, 1974

Throughout the winter of 1974, Senate hearings investigated the corporate practices of the major oil companies operating in the Middle East and charged that a history of either benign government neglect or outright government encouragement had allowed those companies monopoly power over international oil production. In this letter to the editor, one newspaper reader argued that oil companies should either be split up or turned into a public utility, like phone, gas, and water companies at that time.

To the Editor of The Eagle—

Our present status in the energy crisis is much graver than people will let themselves realize. For one thing, 20 major oil companies control almost all of the petroleum in the United States, in any form, from petrochemical manufacturing to gasoline, and fuel oils. Oil imports from Arab countries aren't much more than the oil products being exported from this country to more lucrative markets.

These same companies control two-thirds or better of every other available energy source. These same companies are the only source the federal government has for information on such critical issues as supply and demand, as well as cost and profit. These same companies drop huge sums into the campaigns of certain politicians in order to get opinions in the right places aimed in what they conceive to be the right direction.

"Is Oil a Public Utility?" (letter to the editor), *Berkshire Eagle*, January 11, 1974, p. 14.

I hear about organized crime (i.e., the Mafia, Cosa Nostra, "the Organization"), but has anyone tried to find out why these same companies are responsible for organized famine, organized monopolies, organized profiteering?

What about the daily accounts in the papers and on radio and TV of tankers hanging off the coast until the price is right; unlimited supplies of gasoline for the stations willing to pay the price; 99.9¢-per-gallon stations; mass closings, truck stoppages and cold homes.

If we look at the problems, we find politicians looking the other way, and oil companies emptying the pockets of any and all they can.

Phone companies, power companies, gas and water companies have the power to do the same thing the oil companies are doing; why haven't they? They are publicly owned stock companies that must make a profit for their stockholders just as the oil companies are; where then is the difference?

I submit the difference is the various public utilities commissions. I'm an avid supporter of free enterprise, but what the oil companies are doing isn't free enterprise; it's free back-stabbing aimed at the public. What hurts the most is that the very politicians involved are only in office by the grace of our vote. It's about time we told the politicians what to do—they've been telling us what to do long enough.

I would like either the oil companies broken down into lesser companies wholly separate and independent of each other, or made wholly subject to a public utilities commission or a like body, with rules and regulations just as other utilities. Perhaps then, the free-enterprise system would benefit everyone, not just Shell, Mobil, Exxon, Getty, Arco, Gulf, etc.

BERKSHIRE EAGLE

Lighting the Way for the New Year?

January 7, 1974

In another letter to the Berkshire Eagle, *a woman complained about the "shocking" lack of energy consciousness exhibited by a local store and made a pithy case for the symbolic importance of energy conservation.*

"Lighting the Way for the New Year?" (letter to the editor), *Berkshire Eagle*, January 7, 1974, p. 20.

To the Editor of The Eagle —

I have written as follows to the headquarters office of First National Stores, Inc., in East Hartford. Conn.:

> With shoppers concerned with rising prices and the need for conserving energy, it was a shocking exhibit of corporate indifference for your North Street store in Pittsfield, at 3 P.M. on Dec. 31 to have floodlights blazing from the roof and the exterior walls and parking-lot lights in full force.
>
> I pointed this out to your store manager, Mr. Davey, who explained the lighting goes on automatically.
>
> You set a poor example for housewives who are asked to conserve electricity. You could easily find a way to reset your automatic switch in addition to cutting out every other floodlight.

17

NEW YORK TIMES

Running Out of Gas

January–February 1974

From the moment the Arab oil embargo began, official and unofficial talk circulated about whether the United States would have to ration gasoline. For Americans over the age of forty, rationing brought to mind the gasoline scarcity during World War II, when gas for domestic use was strictly rationed in order to meet military demand. The following documents detail plans laid out — but never implemented — for rationing gasoline, as well as the public fear about fuel scarcity.

WILLIAM ROBBINS

37 Gallons Possible as Monthly Gas Ration

January 21, 1974

*The questions dogged the Nixon administration: Would it resort to gas
rationing, and if so, how severe would it be, and how would it work? By
January 1974, the government had already set in motion the printing of
ration coupons. In the end, however, the administration weathered the
embargo without having to resort to such drastic action. This excerpt
from the* New York Times *explains how the coupons would have worked.*

Eligible drivers in New York City and most of its nearby suburbs
would probably receive about 37 gallons of gasoline a month, under
present projections, if a contingency rationing plan is put into effect
this summer, according to an official of the Federal Energy Office.
Rations could vary from month to month, however, according to available supplies.

The official, John A. Hill, an assistant administrator for policy planning and analysis, explained that the projected gasoline shortfall over
the next few months—the gap between demand and supplies—was
about 1.2 million barrels a day.

While no decision has yet been made to put the rationing plan into
effect, the energy office has said there is a 50-50 chance that rationing
will be needed to prevent intolerably long line-ups at service stations
when demand rises to its normal seasonal peak this summer.

Under the plan, which was published last Monday, all licensed
drivers at least 18 years old would receive coupons, which are being
prepared by the Bureau of Printing and Engraving. . . .

Each coupon book, containing a month's supply, would cost the
driver $1, with the money used to help defray the cost of the program.
The book for each month would remain valid for the following month.

To enable drivers to obtain their coupons, each state would issue
authorization cards on the basis of its list of eligible license-holders.

William Robbins, "37 Gallons Possible as Monthly Gas Ration," *New York Times*, January 21, 1974, p. 14.

The energy office expects to issue the coupons through banks and post offices.

Drivers would not necessarily be limited to the gasoline supplies specified on their coupons because the coupons would be transferable. Officials at the agency predict that if the plan is put into effect, a busy "white market" in coupons will develop.

Mr. Hill explained that 40 percent of the nation's 118 million drivers who would become eligible for rations drove fewer than 5,000 miles a year and that 17 percent drove under 2,500 miles a year. Most of these drivers would have extra coupons that they could sell.

"There is nothing to keep anyone from going into the coupon buying-and-selling business," one official said.

The proposal calls for individual rations to be allocated according to the population density and the availability of mass transit of the area in which each driver lives. There would be no priority classes of drivers of private vehicles.

Even salesmen who must use their cars for work would be given only the standard ration books and would have to depend upon purchases of coupons from the "white market" unless they could establish a hardship case with appeals boards, which would be set up in each county.

PETER KIHSS

Worried Drivers Swamp Stations Selling Gasoline

February 5, 1974

Even though the government never resorted to rationing, gasoline was hard to get. As this document shows, not only were the lines at gas stations long, but Americans also were engaged in panic buying—filling up at every opportunity—out of fear that they would not be able to get gas at some future point. Many states responded to this phenomenon by instituting "odd-even rationing": drivers whose licenses ended in an even number could buy gas on even-numbered days, while drivers with odd-numbered licenses could buy gas on odd-numbered days.

Peter Kihss, "Worried Drivers Swamp Stations Selling Gasoline," *New York Times*, February 5, 1974, p. 20.

Anxious motorists overwhelmed gasoline stations in the metropolitan [New York] area yesterday, with many stations running out of supplies early in the day, while dealers hoped incoming deliveries under February allocations would restore calm by mid-week.

In Brooklyn, Murray Cohen, an owner of the AYS Service Station at Avenue Z and East 17th Street, said he had imposed a $3 maximum for each car's purchases, only to find most people needed only 75 cents' worth to fill up. One man, he said, waited in line for an hour and could use only 35 cents' worth.

In Washington, William E. Simon, director of the Federal Energy Office, who had asked drivers not to buy more than 10 gallons at a time, yesterday issued an appeal to them to stay away from stations unless they bought at least $3 worth.

Car Pooling Stressed

Mr. Simon said he might make the $3 minimum purchase mandatory as soon as Congress enacted legislation giving him such power. "Panic buying isn't helping the situation," he said, contending he had assurances that there would be "enough gasoline if motorists do not use their tanks to hoard."

Gerald J. Turetsky, the regional Federal energy administrator, attributed the renewed gasoline problems both to "panic buying plus late deliveries." Mr. Turetsky declared most gasoline was consumed by commuters, and "as little as a 25 percent increase in car pooling would wipe out the gasoline shortage nationally."

The city's Energy Office, headed by Herbert Elish, reported it was "looking at all suggestions," including plans for minimum purchases, minimum amounts in tanks before purchases and sales of gasoline to cars with even-numbered and odd-numbered license plates on alternate days.

Protection Asked

Some deliveries were interrupted by picketing truck drivers protesting high costs and other problems. The Gulf Oil Corporation said it closed its terminal in Linden, N.J., for the day, cutting off supplies to 120 service stations in the northern third of New Jersey, rather than risk injury or damage, and similarly shut terminals at Neville Island, Delmont, Altoona and Mechanicsburg, Pa., and Huntington, W.Va.

Texaco reported deliveries from Newark and Linden, N.J.; Corapolis, Pa., and Holland, Mich., had been interrupted. It said it had sent telegrams to the Governors of New Jersey and Pennsylvania asking protection for its drivers.

In Perth Amboy, N.J., Police Chief Paul Jankovich reported that windshields had been smashed or tires flattened on 10 trucks at the Chevron refinery. Gulf was able to deliver from its Sewaren terminal, and Exxon said 20 pickets at its Linden plants had not prevented deliveries.

Some retailers complained of excessive cuts in their expected deliveries. Mr. Turetsky said he hoped soon to set up regular monitoring on whether promised allocations were being made "not only by major oil companies, which I believe is the case, but also by distributors."

A check on some complaints by retailers brought oil company explanations to newsmen that, in one case, a new dealer was being allocated gasoline based on sales of his predecessor in the February, 1972, base period, while in another case a station had been counting on supplying new bus customers. In both cases, the companies said, the retailers can file appeals with the Federal Energy Office for increases of up to 10 percent.

County Takes Action

The Board of Chosen Freeholders of Ocean County, which boasts that it is New Jersey's fastest-growing county, with a population of 260,000, obtained a County Court order in Toms River yesterday calling on 10 oil companies to answer complaints of inadequate allocations. Both the county and Toms River town officials had to allocate civil defense supplies of gasoline for emergency vehicles over the weekend.

The Automobile Club of New York said its survey of 97 stations in the city yesterday showed 58 percent had some gasoline. Reporters found long lines of cars throughout the metropolitan area. At least five motorists were reported to have run out of fuel during a 45-minute wait at a Mobil station on Westchester Avenue in White Plains.

At a Citgo station at Broadway and 204th Street, Pat LaFalce, the owner, said he did have gasoline but had shut off his pumps deliberately so that he could "get my mechanical work done in the garage."

A 45-mile drive indicated that only 10 to 15 percent of the stations in Queens were pumping gasoline. Of 30 stations, 14 were out of gasoline, and a few others were serving only regular customers, a practice barred in New York City by a regulation that has drawn station complaints.

3

Oil, Consumption, and the Environment

As the previous documents have shown, Americans understood the oil crisis in a variety of ways. They differed in terms of how they perceived the threats and dangers that had led up to and were produced by OPEC's decisions in October 1973, and they differed in terms of the hardships on which they focused. Nevertheless, a consistent feature of the public dialogue about the crisis was the way it plugged into nascent environmental concerns.

While other "oil shocks" followed this first one in 1973, the Arab oil embargo's impact on the United States was magnified by its timing with the rapidly growing environmental movement of the early 1970s. Although activists concerned with the environmental health of the planet had been around for a while, by most accounts the galvanizing event that formed a truly *national* environmental movement was the disaster that occurred off the coast of Santa Barbara, California, on January 28, 1969. When workers on a Union Oil Company platform were replacing a drill bit, mounting pressure beneath the ocean floor caused a "blowout," ultimately spilling more than 3 million gallons of oil (as well as natural gas) into the ocean. The blowout created an eight-hundred-square-mile oil slick and caused oil to wash up on thirty-five miles of California beaches.

Although the Santa Barbara spill affected a relatively small number of people, it provoked congressional hearings and intense public commentary, and it helped usher in a period of profound public criticism of the oil industry. It also motivated legislators to take note of the environment. At the federal level, Congress passed the National Environmental Policy Act of 1970 and the Clean Water Acts of 1972. At the state level, California passed a number of environmental laws that sought to protect the state's coastline. The growth of the environmental movement was perhaps best symbolized by the fact that millions of Americans celebrated the nation's first Earth Day on April 22, 1970.

As a result, concerns about oil pollution became connected with a wider set of environmental issues and agendas. Many new voices emerged, describing what environmentalists saw as the grim future for human beings if they did not take the environment into greater consideration. Among these voices were a number of scientists and policy scholars who turned their attention to analyzing the costs and burdens of postwar development. Few people did more to provide the public with a scientifically grounded picture of global environmental problems than Barry Commoner. Commoner was one of the first people to link American technologies used to wage war in Vietnam with environmental devastation both in Southeast Asia and at home. The production of chemicals such as Agent Orange, used to defoliate trees and destroy food crops in Vietnam, resulted not only in a toxic overload for those exposed to it but also dangerous levels of toxic waste in its production. Beginning in the 1960s, Commoner became one of the most thoughtful critics of modern industrial society, and his sense that the environment could no longer support modern human life at its current pace was widely shared, as evidenced by the documents in this chapter.

From another corner of academia, in 1972 a group of scientists at the Massachusetts Institute of Technology (MIT) wrote a book titled *Limits to Growth,* which served as a kind of slogan for the way many Americans envisioned the future. Using newly developed computer models, the authors argued that no matter what area of human life one examined—resource development, agriculture, population growth—precarious scenarios emerged in which humans would face chronic shortages and crises if they did not develop more sustainable forms of technology. Although other scientists exposed serious flaws in the authors' modeling, such pessimistic views became relatively common currency during the early 1970s, as mainstream magazines and newspapers featured repeated stories on environmental problems.

The documents that follow show a range of environmentalist responses, as well as one skeptic's retort, to the problems that faced Americans in the early 1970s. Document 23, written in the midst of the oil embargo, echoes in tone and in substance environmentalists' views of what they thought the United States should do to solve the wider energy crisis—of which the embargo was, they argued, just one part.

18

DAVID PERLMAN

America the Beautiful?

November 4, 1969

In this article from the popular magazine Look, *science journalist David Perlman began with an image that stunned many people in 1969: the vision of earth from space. Never before had humans glimpsed their planet from afar. Now, with the Apollo space missions, people could see the earth for what it was—a finite planetary body seemingly floating in space. Perlman touched on many of the environmental themes that concerned Americans at the end of the 1960s—most prominently, whether technological advancement was fundamentally endangering the ecological health of the planet.*

This year [1969] America took a firsthand look at the moon. But in years to come, 1969 may best be remembered as the year of our first long view of America the Beautiful and the rest of our earth. The Apollo capsules, invisible in the vastness of space, broadcasting television images back to American viewers, became mirrors in which we could see ourselves anew. It was a humbling experience.

From Apollo, the receding earth looked as lonely in space as the spacecraft seemed from earth. Suddenly, we could understand what Adlai Stevenson had said:[1]

> We travel together, passengers on a little spaceship; dependent on its vulnerable reserves of air and soil; all committed for our safety to its security and peace; preserved from annihilation only by the care, the work and . . . the love we give our fragile craft.

[1]*Adlai Stevenson*: Democratic candidate for president in 1952 and 1956; appointed as U.S. ambassador to the United Nations in 1961. He gave the speech that is quoted in Perlman's article at the Economic and Social Council of the United Nations in Geneva shortly before his death in July 1965. [Ed.]

David Perlman, "America the Beautiful?" *Look*, November 4, 1969, 25–27.

The earth was revealed as Apollo's twin: Spaceship Earth. Man on one spaceship radioed to man on the other: "The earth from here is a grand oasis in the . . . vastness of space!" An oasis: a fragile outpost of life in a lifeless pocket of the universe. But the astronauts, sustained by their intricate, perfectly functioning man-made life systems, could see signs of trouble in the more complex, natural life systems of Spaceship Earth.

The Apollo 10 astronauts, looking down on America the Beautiful, easily picked out Los Angeles. Even from orbit, they recognized its sink of whiskey-brown smog, where 4 million cars vomit unburned hydrocarbons, tetraethyl lead and cancer-causing nickel additives; where 16 million rubber tires vaporize on the abrading freeways and invisible but deadly asbestos particles shed from brake linings.

In orbit, the astronauts passed over other trouble spots, spreading cancerlike in the "oasis" of earth below. Everywhere are the works of modern man, yet all his technology—products of the same genius that created the spaceship's perfect environment—has neither created a fit environment for the human community nor preserved the precious diversity and plenty of the other organisms with which man shares this planet.

Indeed, the impact of technology on the earth's ecology—the indivisible web of life—threatens the continued existence of life itself. The life-support system of Spaceship Earth is no less fragile than that of Apollo. Applied without wisdom or prudence, the same technology that is our servant may prove to be our ultimate executioner. This Jekyll-to-Hyde switch is most evident in America, the citadel of modern technology, but the same phenomenon has been spreading all around the world, keeping step with what we self-deceptively call progress.

Off Bermuda, a rocky islet stands in the Atlantic. It harbors one hundred sea-feeding petrels, birds that never touch a continental land mass. A gentle dust, windblown from North African croplands three thousand miles away, falls to the ocean and poisons fish with DDT from the dust motes. The Bermuda petrels, last of their species, feed on the fish and lay eggs that never hatch. Extinction is near for the petrel. Other species face the same fate.

Eastward across the Atlantic, the Algerian Sahara is spotted with the ragged green of date-palm groves. Two thousand wells lower underground water levels, and a million date palms die. The sands advance, threatening the livelihood of 120,000 desert dwellers.

Eastward still, the sands and salt marshes of Southern Iraq reveal how long men have plundered this planet. Ur of the Chaldees towered here above all other cities in the days of Abraham; but the exploited earth struck back, dams and canals silted up. For two thousand years, the land of Ur has been almost as dead as the moon.

Vast India, a nation only twenty years old, takes seven minutes to cross by satellite. Its troubles scar the land with a havoc of numbers: eight sprawling cities with up to 5 million underfed humans in each; a bursting population of 550 million that grows by 12 to 13 million a year, while valiant but futile family-planning campaigns touch 3 to 4 million at best.

Beyond Asia, the blue of oceans seems unmarred for seven thousand miles. Yet on islands below, phosphate mining, bomb testing and lagoon draining have destroyed fragile ecosystems and driven away whole communities of men and animals. In the creatures of the sea, new man-made chemicals, like a time bomb, are working their way through nucleus and fat body, oviduct and bloodstream, ready for a reckoning.

In Egypt, the great mainstream of the Nile river, its mouths emptying into the Mediterranean, is now controlled by the Aswan High Dam, more than six hundred miles upstream from the sea. Three miles across, the massive dam impounds a lake three hundred miles long, and growing. Dr. Mohammed Abdul-Fattah al Kassas of the University of Cairo tells how Aswan has slowed the Nile's downstream flow so that protective dunes and sandbars no longer build up along the delta shore to fend off the invading sea. The Mediterranean is flooding in on the delta, and one million acres of fertile farmlands are disappearing under salt water. The village where Dr. al Kassas was born is now buried beneath the sea, two miles out from the delta's new shoreline. And on the surface of vast Lake Nasser, above the Aswan dam, wild water hyacinths that evaporate water into the air are spreading. The lake may lose as much water by evaporation each year as it is supposed to send down the Nile for irrigation. But poisoning the hyacinths would mean poisoning the lake.

Dr. Henry van der Schalie, University of Michigan zoologist and veteran disease fighter in Egypt's villages, predicts that snails carrying the wormlike blood flukes of schistosomiasis will soon infest five hundred miles of new irrigation canals below Aswan. Peasants irrigating land from these new canals, he says, will succumb to the painful and virtually incurable disease.

Aswan is already a liability for Egypt's fishermen, according to Dr. Carl J. George of Union College. The flooding Nile used to carry 50 to 100 million tons of nutrient-rich sediments a year out to sea, but the nutrients no longer flow, and the fish catch has collapsed. The economic loss is $7 million a year, and Egyptian fishing families have abandoned their rake-sailed feluccas for the indifferent slums of Alexandria and Cairo.

Aswan is a bitter example of "ecological backlash," in the phrase of Dr. Barry Commoner of Washington University. Other so-called technological triumphs are setting off a backlash all over the world. In Santa Barbara, for example, the Union Oil Company's new offshore well has spilled some 3.5 million gallons of crude petroleum into the sea since last January [1969] when drilling operations created a leak in the undersea rock structure. Until that geological formation empties, oil will continue to push up through ancient earthquake fissures, even if it's pumped, and the beaches and birds of the Santa Barbara channel will be threatened. It may last twenty years. Already, entire populations of seabirds—cormorants, grebes and mergansers—have been destroyed by the upwelling oil. Kelp beds have suffocated, and tidal plankton has been killed. Clinging to particles of sediment, tons of oil have sunk. No one knows what damage is done to fragile species of sea-bottom organisms with which the whole cycle of oceanic life is linked.

Aquatic life suffers from too much heat—thermal pollution—as well as from oil. Most power plants—nuclear or conventional—burn fuel to heat water to turn turbines to generate electricity. Hot waste water is dumped into streams and oceans; many fish die under a temperature rise of only a few degrees, and the aquatic ecosystem shifts abruptly.

Land and water can die from other ecological time bombs. Excess fertilizers standing on farm fields sterilize the soil; runoff pollutes waterways with nitrates. Phosphates have overnourished Lake Erie to death. Two thousand silt-filled irrigation dams in America stand useless, while upstream banks erode. Strip mining in Missouri, Kentucky, Illinois and West Virginia has left vicious, unhealing scars on the land and damaged thirteen thousand miles of streams through acid drainage. In Hudspeth County, Texas, below El Paso on the Rio Grande, secondhand irrigation water is so salty the Federal Land Bank sells abandoned farms, once valued at $1,000 an acre, for $50 an acre.

If these were isolated instances of technological error, they could be written off as the price of progress, regrettable but unavoidable. But as human population increases and technology improves, man in his ecological blindness is suicidally attacking the foundation of life itself. . . .

Biologist Barry Commoner, predicting imminent worldwide famine, speaks of the biosphere as man's most important machine:

> This machine is our biological capital, the basic apparatus on which our total productivity depends. If we destroy it, our most advanced technology will come to naught, and any economic and political systems that depend on it will flounder. Yet the major threat to the integrity of this biological capital is technology itself. . . . Technological advances have proved to be powerful intrusions on geophysical and ecological systems. Most of our difficulties result from the failure to recognize this basic fact in time. The failing may become fatal as we progress to the vast new development necessary to avert the impending world famine.

Despite such pleas for an ecological approach to development, huge projects are still planned and executed without adequate study of their effects on the environment.

One of many experiments on the drawing boards is a badly needed new canal at sea level across the Isthmus of Panama. The Atomic Energy Commission is examining the feasibility of blasting out the canal with strings of buried thermonuclear explosives totaling 250 megatons or more in energy yield. This would far exceed the power of all the nuclear bombs ever tested—more force than two or three San Francisco earthquakes. These crater-digging devices would send fallout clouds forty thousand feet high; "short term" radiation hazards would require evacuating tens of thousands of Central American Indians from jungle villages and coastal fishing communities for up to two years. The ecological effects could be monumental. But even if the new Panama canal is not dug by nuclear explosives, the fact that it will run across the Isthmus at sea level rather than through a series of locks fills the project with unknowns. For no one can predict the effect of abruptly mixing the waters of two great oceans after they have been separated throughout four million years of geologic time.

What will happen when tidal surges in the Pacific, eighteen feet higher than the Atlantic, rush across the Isthmus bearing millions of tons of water with a different salinity, a different temperature, a different population of marine organisms? Thousands of species of sea animals may become extinct under the new marine environment. Climate may alter; the lives of nations may be blindly transformed.

The world ecosystems—the networks of organisms, from microbes to man, that live in precarious balance—are fragile indeed. Water, air, open space, living plants and living animals are all essential; we break their cycles, and sunder the web of life, at our peril. Do we act now to restore a livable environment to our planet, or do we allow the explosion of human numbers and the technological disruption of our global ecosystem to continue without forethought or control? Isaiah the prophet cried out when the desert sands, sterilized by generations of exploitation, were already advancing on Ur of the Chaldees and on the fertile fields outside Jerusalem:

> The earth also is defiled under the inhabitants thereof . . .
> Therefore the inhabitants of the earth are burned, and few men
>   left. . . .
> And all her princes shall be nothing.
> And thorns shall come up in her palaces, nettles and brambles in
>   the fortresses thereof; and it shall be an habitation of dragons,
>   and a court for owls. [Isaiah 24:5, 6; 34:12, 13]

Two thousand six hundred years later, Albert Schweitzer,[2] looking around at the Africa he loved and healed, echoed Isaiah:

"Man has lost the capacity to foresee and to forestall. He will end by destroying the earth."

---

[2] *Albert Schweitzer:* Prominent doctor and humanitarian who was awarded the Nobel Peace Prize in 1952. [Ed.]

19

NORMAN PODHORETZ

Doomsday Fears and Modern Life

October 1971

The environmental movement received its share of criticism, and one of the most common remarks heard in the early 1970s (as well as today) was that environmentalists saw doom and gloom everywhere they looked. For Norman Podhoretz, editor of the neoconservative magazine Commentary, *such dim visions revealed an irrational apocalypticism that had its roots in Americans' fear of nuclear war in the 1950s. Writing that most people in the world seemed ready to embrace "the benefits of life in an advanced industrial society," Podhoretz argued that there was no turning back the clock.*

For . . . [one] strain of apocalyptic thinking which has been gathering force and influence in the last few years, . . . the human species has reached a point at which it is about to destroy itself altogether and quite possibly the entire planet as well. The contemporary avatar of this ancient expectation of an imminent End of Days was given a powerful stimulus by the invention of nuclear weapons, and if not for one of the most curious and least remarked developments of the curious age in which we live, it might well have gone on indefinitely looking to the mushroom cloud for the perverse comfort a great anxiety always finds in the thought that its fears are real. The curious development was that everyone suddenly stopped believing in the possibility of a major nuclear war.

When exactly, this astonishing change occurred, or why it should have occurred at all, would be very hard to say; conceivably it was an effect of the Cuban missile crisis. But whatever the reasons may be, there is no question that very few people still seriously fear the eruption of a major nuclear war between the United States and the Soviet Union or for that matter between the United States and China—the

Norman Podhoretz, "Doomsday Fears and Modern Life," *Commentary*, October 1971, 4, 6.

kind of war that used to be associated with visions of the end of the world and that was so recently considered by so many to be a virtual inevitability. It is true that the idea of a limited nuclear war between Israel and Egypt or even between the Soviet Union and China still seems plausible, but such a war, whether rightly or wrongly, is no longer commonly imagined to spell the end of the world.

The fascinating consequence is that we rarely find any great emphasis being put on nuclear war nowadays by the catastrophist schools of apocalyptic thought. They mention it, of course, they trot it out and bow to it and pay it their obeisance. But they do so in a spirit of perfunctory piety which perfectly expresses their recognition that it has all at once become a doddering presence in the contemporary imagination, that it has lost its power to convince. For the moment at least, that power has passed to pollution. Technology is destroying ecology and will end by destroying us all: so, stated in the most general terms, runs the formula which in not much more than a year or two has won a most amazing degree of uncritical acceptance in every circle and on every side.

Thus ideas which only yesterday would have been dismissed as crackpot are today given a respectful hearing. There is, for example, the theory that thermal pollution is melting the polar ice cap by slow but inexorable degrees, so that the end of the world will come by flood (in direct contravention of the biblical promise expressed in the symbol of the rainbow). Or, on the contrary, we are told that the rays of the sun are being effectively blocked by the pollution of the air, so that the end of the world will come by frost. More plausibly E. J. Mishan, a catastrophist who has nothing whatever of the crackpot in him, warns of "the chances of extinction of our species from uncontrolled epidemics caused by the deadlier viruses that have evolved in response to widespread application of new 'miracle' drugs, or from some ecological calamity caused by our inadvertent destruction of those forms of animal and insect life that once preyed on the pests that consumed men's harvests."

Professor Mishan, unlike some others among us of an apocalyptic bent of mind, is well aware that "the belief that the end of the world was drawing nigh has been widely held at different times in human history." But he will allow no consolation to be gained from this, for the "doomsday fears of yesterday had no rational basis" while "those of today have plenty." This seems to me an amazingly arrogant statement, especially coming from a writer who professes in other contexts to have so little faith in the superiority of the modern understanding of the mysteries of life on this planet to the wisdoms of "yesterday." The truth is that the doomsday fears of today have as much or as little rational basis as doomsday fears ever did, if by rational we mean subject to scientific proof. No proof exists that the end of the world is at hand. We do not even have persuasive evidence pointing to that conclusion. All we have, exactly as the men of yesterday did, are warnings and exhortations to the effect that we are doomed unless we repent and change our ways and return to the proper path. That such warnings and exhortations are often voiced by professional scientists and couched in the language of science does not in the least endow them with the authority of tested scientific statements. When they speak of these matters, the scientists in question are speaking not as scientists but as moralists and ideologues, and no one ought to be fooled.

But if there is no rational basis for the apocalypticism of Mishan and others, neither is Sir Peter Medawar[1] right on the other side in asserting that "the deterioration of the environment produced by technology is a technological problem for which technology has found, is finding, and will continue to find solutions." Even setting aside the interesting theoretical question of how a problem which is by definition a consequence of the growth of technology can be solved by the further growth of technology, one must still reject the notion—so characteristic of a certain type of liberal mentality—that anything can be had for nothing provided the right formula or gimmick or gadget can be found. Surely where the benefits of technology are concerned, as with human affairs in all of their many modalities, there will always be a price to pay, and the price will always be high, and justly high in the case of technology considering what it can buy. The air of industrial societies will never be as sweet as the air of a mountain retreat; cities will never afford the "margin, space, ease and openness" for which critics like Mishan so eloquently yearn, however lacking in eloquence and however philistine the spirit in which they speak of the gains in freedom of every kind—from want, from disease, from tribal coercion, from claustrophobia—that are purchased, most willingly and eagerly by most people the minute they are given the chance, through the sacrifice of other undoubted goods to the gods of advanced modernity.

---

[1] *Sir Peter Medawar*: British immunologist who was awarded the Nobel Prize in Medicine in 1960. [Ed.]

In saying that there will always be a price for technology, and that the price will always be high, I do not by any means wish to suggest that it cannot be lowered to some extent or that technology itself cannot be employed to that end. For it is undoubtedly true that some of the dangerous and unpleasant consequences of technology can be softened or even eliminated by technological means. Ways can be found of producing energy that are less damaging to the environment than traditional methods have been (though there is always the likelihood that these new methods will take their toll on different features of the environment than present methods do). Factories and automobiles and airplanes can in fact be equipped with devices—technological devices—that cut down on the volume of noxious material they pour into the atmosphere; streams and rivers already polluted can in fact be cleaned up and the air can be cleaned up too (though there is always the likelihood that all this can only be accomplished at the expense of other social and even ecological goods). Nevertheless, as much of this kind of thing as can be done should be done, just as at an earlier stage of industrial development certain necessary measures were taken in the field of sanitation and in the field of public health.

It is precisely here that the damaging effects of the apocalyptic perspective make themselves most vividly felt. On the issue of the environment, as on so many other issues, the prophets of doom are often excused or even praised on the ground that they "wake people up" to the existence of a problem and therefore contribute to the mobilization of the political will necessary to work toward solutions. My own observation is that, on the contrary, prophecies of doom are more likely to put people to sleep than to wake them up: why bother striving if the end is in sight? And when it is not serving to induce apathy, the apocalyptic perspective is serving to prepare for and justify the institution of extraordinary measures of political control. For to announce the apocalypse is, at bottom, to declare a state of emergency, and the suspension of normal liberties is one of the first things that happens when a state of emergency is declared. On this account alone, if for no other reason, any alarmist or catastrophist view of any public problem—especially one so fundamental as the survival of the species itself—ought to be received with the greatest skepticism, and the heaviest burden of proof put on anyone who wishes to persuade us that we are doomed unless we radically change our ways. In the face of the clear eagerness of the vast majority of people—not just in the

Western countries, but everywhere, all over the world—to acquire or hold on to the benefits of life in an advanced industrial society, and in the face of their obvious willingness to pay even an exorbitant price, only the most extreme measures of political, social, and moral coercion could accomplish the kind of reversal of the forces of technological growth which the apocalyptic critics tell us is our only alternative to doom.

For myself I believe in the existence of a third alternative which is to accept modern society, with its imperatives of restless growth, as a *viable* human possibility superior to some the world has seen and inferior to others but in any case a viable possibility and a *natural* one: a poor thing, perhaps, but our own. It is the way into which *we* were born and the way in which we are going to die, and it is the way in which, between those two points, we have to make a life. To make a life is to strike a continuing series of bargains—with nature, with the past, with the future—and to make a good life is to make the soundest and fairest bargains we can. This is not what the apocalyptic perspective asks us or encourages us to do, but it is the best we can do and it probably is all we should ever even try.

20

JOHN NOBLE WILFORD

Questioning Economic Growth

July 8, 1971

One of the most profound challenges raised by the environmental movement was its questioning of the value of economic growth. Although the United States had already established itself as a worldwide commercial power in the late nineteenth century, after World War II it experienced unprecedented economic expansion. Throughout the 1960s, people began

John Noble Wilford, "The Nation's Energy Crisis: Is Unbridled Growth Indispensable to the Good Life?" *New York Times*, July 8, 1971, p. 24.

raising concerns about the environmental costs that such a driving emphasis on the economy produced. In this excerpt, New York Times *science writer and two-time Pulitzer Prize winner John Noble Wilford explored how an energy crisis might reshape American attitudes toward economic matters and, particularly, toward the federal government's relationship to the economy.*

In searching for ways to meet the nation's soaring energy needs without damaging the environment, some American experts are beginning to question one of this country's most cherished beliefs: the idea that boundless economic growth is indispensable to the good life.

If the environment is finite, according to these social scientists, engineers, economists and environmentalists, then perhaps economic growth has its limits too, particularly the unbridled growth that has characterized the United States almost from the start.

What those limits are, or more specifically how a slow-growth economy would be managed and what the social and political implications of such a policy of national planning might be, are questions that the critics of growth have given little detailed thought to.

But they agree that the changes needed to contain the energy crisis may well prove to be radical since, if the logic of the situation is carried to its end, whoever sets priorities for energy consumption wields enormous power over the economy and over the entire national life style.

They are convinced, in any case, that change of some sort will be essential. As Dr. Barry Commoner, an outspoken Washington University biologist, asserts: "The environment got there first, and it's up to the economic system to adjust to the environment. Any economic system must be compatible with the environment, or it will not survive."

Controlling growth, economists say, would confront the nation with a host of difficult problems. Unemployment could rise. The poor could be locked in their poverty. Education, research and cultural pursuits might suffer. The nation could lose economic and political stature.

Millions of individual decisions traditionally made through the random choices of consumers and the supply-and-demand forces of a relatively uncontrolled economy would have to be passed upward to the national level and made through some form of comprehensive national planning.

Most authorities agree that such far-reaching Government power would run against the American grain and that the American people would not easily accept more controls unless the energy crisis got much worse. What the critics of growth are saying, in a word, is that the crisis *is* getting worse, and rapidly.

Consumption of all energy sources is rising between 3 and 4 percent a year, which is faster than population increases and basic economic growth. By the year 2000, according to some projections, there will be 320 million Americans (compared to 203 million now), and they may be using three or four times the current energy output. Hardly a shore or river bank would be without a power plant every few miles.

"We're not pessimists or doom-mongers. We just see technological reasons to do some new social thinking," says Dr. John List, assistant professor of engineering at the California Institute of Technology's new Environmental Quality Laboratory.

> We've got about twenty years in which to reorganize [Dr. List continues]. Population growth hardly comes into it at all. It's growth in per capita consumption. It's just plain affluence. The only way out of it that we can see is to curb the energy consumption per person. Not exactly a no-growth situation, but slow it down from this 9 percent [growth-rate] madness.

. . . When slow-growth or no-growth ideas are raised, businessmen, economists and engineers usually react with variations of the time-honored principle that growth is progress and progress is good. They stand firm on the premise reflected by John L. O'Sullivan, the American editor credited with coining the expansionist expression "manifest destiny." Said Mr. O'Sullivan in 1845: "The only healthy state of a nation is perpetual growth."

But a crisis, if not completely catastrophic, can change thinking patterns and give impetus to social invention, as the economic crisis of the Depression years did in this country. To ecologists, such radical thinking is once again a necessity.

One of the basic laws of the biosphere is that energy, when expended, ends up as heat—the warmth of a stove or light bulb, the blast of an industrial furnace, the heat of an auto engine and the heat emitted by power-plant stacks and cooling waters.

In power plants, conventional or nuclear, only 30 to 40 percent of the fuel's heat is converted to electricity, and engineers doubt there can be any significant improvements in efficiency for at least two or three decades. Consequently, some 60 percent of the heat is released in a concentrated dose at the power-plant site and the other 40 percent over the points of use, primarily the urban areas.

At some point, scientists caution, the cumulative effects of power generation could alter global climate.

21

WILLIAM K. STEVENS

Rush to Smaller Cars Spurs Detroit to Alter Assembly Lines

December 3, 1973

To Americans and non-Americans alike, nothing spoke so much to the nation's love of consumption more than the car. Detroit was the birthplace of the automobile industry and the world's center of automobile manufacturing. The problem was that in the fall of 1973, Detroit had relatively little to offer consumers looking for fuel efficiency. Long in the business of building big cars with powerful engines and roomy insides, American automakers were caught off-guard by the oil crisis, especially as consumers began turning either to compact American models—which were less profitable for the manufacturers—or to German and Japanese cars that got better gas mileage. But producing smaller cars involved a significant restructuring of the American automobile industry, as the following article explains.

Suddenly, in the last month or so, the energy crisis has caused the trend toward smaller, less extravagant cars to surge ahead faster than anyone had expected. And the auto industry is scrambling to catch up.

So dramatic has been the shift that some industry leaders are

William K. Stevens, "Rush to Smaller Cars Spurs Detroit to Alter Assembly Lines," *New York Times*, December 3, 1973, p. 48.

beginning to wonder whether the American attachment to the big automobile as status symbol might be lessening drastically, perhaps permanently, in the face of hard necessity.

Caught with too few assembly lines set up for compact and subcompact cars, the Big three auto makers are hurrying to convert big-car lines, at an estimated cost of $500 million.

Left holding a surplus of gasoline-gulping standard-size cars that have been shunned by buyers newly conscious of fuel economy, General Motors and Chrysler are temporarily shutting down 18 big-car assembly plants.

Looking for Small Cars

Out in the marketplace, used-car dealers are frantically trying to lay their hands on small cars; so much so that a subcompact Pinto sold at wholesaler's auction here is commanding a price about equal to that of a full-size Impala in comparable condition.

Industry analysts believe that within the near future, perhaps by next fall, compacts and subcompacts for the first time will account for 50 percent of the new-car market. Ford expects by next spring to have converted half its manufacturing capacity to small cars.

Most analysts had expected the 50 percent goal to be reached several years from now as the small-car trend that started in the 1960s continued to grow. As the 1970s began, 26 percent of all new cars were compacts or subcompacts. During the 1973 model year just ended, the figure grew to 40 percent.

Thousands Face Layoffs

Before the current short-term scramble to accelerate small-car production is over, thousands of workers on big-car assembly lines will have been laid off their jobs for brief periods. And although some auto executives do not foresee any big layoff as a direct result of the gasoline shortage, fears are growing about a general recession caused partly by the energy crisis. For in Detroit, a saying is that if the economy catches a cold, the auto industry develops pneumonia.

Further, the current situation may well alter the short-term competitive balance within the industry. Ford and American Motors are in the happy position of having emphasized smaller cars this year, while General Motors and Chrysler have not.

"The days of the standard cars in high volume are over," William A.

McNamee, Ford's recently designated energy planning manager, said the other day.

Chrysler Figures

Sales figures from Chrysler for the 10-day period ending Nov. 20 are illustrative:

Full-size Dodge Monaco, down from 3,402 to 2,052 units, or 33 percent, as compared with the same period a year ago. Compact Dodge Dart, up from 6.059 to 7.544, or 25 percent. Full-size Plymouth Fury, down 36 percent. Compact Plymouth Valiant, up 31 percent.

Only one segment of the big-car market—the super-luxury cars such as the Cadillac, Continental and Imperial—has held steady. The reasoning in the industry is that people who buy such cars are going to buy them come what may.

Some auto dealers see an element of panic—even foolishness—in the way some car owners are reacting. Some big-car owners are merely stepping down one notch to intermediate-size cars. Industry studies show, however, that there is not much difference in fuel economy between full-size and intermediate.

"The intelligent people are buying subcompacts or foreign cars," said an Oldsmobile dealer in Grosse Pointe. "The not so intelligent are being panicked into buying intermediates."

A General Motors study of fuel economy among a representative group of 1974 cars indicates that an owner who switches from a standard-size car to a compact typically will use about 10 percent less gas when driving in city traffic and about 12 percent less on the open highway. If he switches to a subcompact, he will use about 40 percent less gas in town, about 30 [percent] less on the road.

Industry sources say that although buyers are going smaller, they are not so willing to give up options, comfort and styling in doing so. That is all right with the industry, because that is one way in which it makes profits.

Ford finds itself in the fortunate position of having come out this year with its four-cylinder Mustang II, a small car with luxury trim, options and interior.

Even though Ford's Rouge plant is working full blast and turning out 72 Mustangs an hour 20 hours a day, it cannot build enough of them and other small cars. Nor can any of the other auto makers. And that has occasioned the middle-of-the-year drive to convert as many big-car plants as possible to small-car production.

Chrysler announced this week that beginning Jan. 16, its Newark, Del., assembly plant, one of three big-car plants Chrysler owns, would begin producing compact Darts and Valiants instead of standard-size Monacos and Furies. Ford and General Motors announced similar conversions earlier, effective soon after the first of the year.

To "balance inventories" that are too heavily loaded with big cars, GM plans to shut down 16 big-car assembly plants during the week of Dec. 17, and Chrysler will close its two large-car plants for three days early in January.

These measures are seen as the major short-term adjustment that industry can make. Some cars may be modified to improve gas mileage—for example, by installing smaller engines, trimming weight slightly and adjusting gear ratios. But industry spokesmen say that many such adjustments must meet Federal pollution control standards, standards that are now being reconsidered by Congress with the aim of saving fuel.

No Changes Till '78

And because it takes a long time to design an automobile, no major design changes to improve fuel economy are envisioned before the 1976 models at the earliest.

There is one exception, however. When most of the 1975 models come out next fall, they will be equipped with an antipollution device called the catalytic converter. Use of the converter will enable the auto companies to retune automobile engines, and this could improve gas economy. General Motors expects it to improve by 13 percent, the other auto companies by considerably less or not at all.

What the accelerated small-car boom will mean to the relative competitive positions of the Big Four auto makers is not entirely clear. But it is evident that both Ford and American Motors have been presented with an opportunity to make inroads in the market if they can exploit it.

American Motors has been building only small cars for some years and now finds that segment of the market golden.

"If we could build them, we could sell them," says Gerald C. Meyers, an American Motors vice president.

Restyling Big Cars

Chrysler, faced with limited resources, decided in 1969 to increase big-car production for 1974 rather than bring out a subcompact car. It spent $400 million to restyle its large-car production, only to run into the present crunch.

The energy crisis has had its impact on the industry in other ways. The general scarcity of energy is expected to hit the auto factories hard.

More immediate, perhaps, is a materials shortage related partly to the scarcity of oil. Modern automobiles contain many parts made of plastic, and plastic is derived from petroleum. In addition, many parts producers have said they are unwilling to expand their plants because of the generally uncertain energy and economic climate.

A widespread parts shortage has therefore developed. American Motors says this, rather than assembly plant capacity, is limiting its production. Chrysler announced last week that four compact car plants would close for three days early in January because of a lack of parts.

Problem of Layoffs

What effect on the employees these and other plant closings and slow-downs will have is not entirely clear, either. Under the union contracts, workers with at least a year's seniority get 95 percent of their take-home pay when they are faced with such layoffs. Edward N. Cole, General Motors president, said this week that he did not expect any substantial layoffs during 1974. However, overtime work—eagerly sought by many employees because it is so lucrative—certainly will be cut, if not eliminated, at many plants.

Is there to be a drastic falling-off of production in the industry in 1974, after a 1973 in which a record 11.5 million cars and trucks will have rolled off the assembly lines?

"We're optimistic we can avoid one," said Mr. McNamee of Ford. "We've been operating at such high levels that we can retreat quite a way and still be operating at 'normal' levels. We could drop back to 10.5 [million vehicles produced] and it would still be the second largest year in history."

22

TIME

The Big Car: End of the Affair

December 31, 1973

Although Americans have long loved big cars, the high price of gasoline and the poor economy forced people to reevaluate their consumer choices over the course of 1973, especially after the Arab oil embargo. But as this cover from Time indicates, the end of Americans' "affair" with big, low-mileage cars was a painful one for both consumers and producers. As the previous document indicated, the oil crisis forced American automakers to redesign their manufacturing process, and American consumers turned reluctantly to smaller vehicles. By 1974, fuel efficiency did indeed become a major selling point in the automobile industry, but only if car manufacturers could package a car's "mpg" in ways that would appeal to Americans, namely, by also emphasizing engine power and roominess.

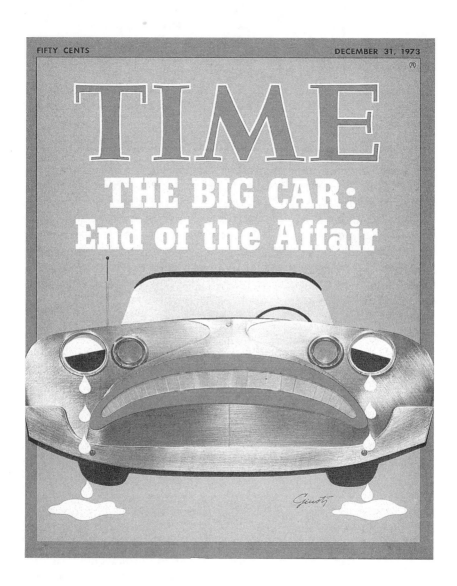

23

ANTHONY WAYNE SMITH

The Oil Shortage

February 1974

For many environmentalists, the problem with OPEC and Middle Eastern oil supplies was simply one aspect of a larger issue: Americans' dependence on fossil fuels. Environmentalists had voiced their concerns about oil consumption in the years before the oil crisis, but during and after the Arab oil embargo, they spoke with even greater fervor about the need for the United States to develop an ecologically sound energy policy. In this piece, the president of the National Parks Association, an advocacy group, detailed the sweeping transformations he and other environmentalists believed were necessary to save the country.

The energy crisis confronts the American people with a need to correct the gross mismanagement of the economy which has been rampant for much too long.

The mismanagement centers at the moment in the liquid-fuels and motor-transportation segment of the economy, but is not confined to that segment.

The structured portion of the economy, consisting of the large corporations and the symbiotic government agencies, is planned and controlled in the manner of oligopoly by corporate management. The difficulty does not lie in the lack of industrywide planning nor even of interindustry coordination, bad as that has been, but in the values which govern the planning.

The goals of industrial planning have been growth, power, and money (not necessarily profit for stockholders, but executive salaries and bonuses). It should now be apparent that growth as a value must yield to a differential stabilization. While profitability is a necessary value (even in most public enterprises in the long run, but depending

Anthony Wayne Smith, "The Oil Shortage," *National Parks and Conservation Magazine*, February 1974, 2, 35.

on how you measure it), the values of ecological security and social relevance must shortly be added, if we are to escape disintegration. There are plenty of ways in a democratic society to compel such reforms.

Consider the record in the oil matter to date. The corporations themselves held up the construction of the Alaskan pipeline for four years by (1) the blundering and irresponsible choice of an unecological route, (2) the acceptance of construction permits in violation of law with respect to the width of the right-of-way and the requirement of adequate environmental impact statements, and (3) their refusal to consider alternative routes.

The environmental movement did *not* oppose the extraction of oil from the Arctic pools, but insisted quite properly that the laws be obeyed and the alternatives be considered. . . .

Nor will the flow of crude oil from the Arctic, when it comes, redress the shortage; the demand and the costs will be too high. And the first big pipeline break and spill, which will certainly ensue from the inevitable earthquake along the Denali fault, or the first supertanker disaster in the stormy waters of the Gulf of Alaska will reopen the whole environmental question.

It is the corporations themselves that have delayed the tapping of the oil pools under the continental shelves. The blame for the Santa Barbara catastrophe and the fires and spills in the Gulf of Mexico does not rest upon the public, but on corporate management. The communities and industries along our coasts will never again tolerate the befouling of their shorelines as a consequence of pollution from drilling or from ships.

For quite a long time the diagrams, whether done by hand or by computer, have been forecasting the exhaustion of domestic petroleum resources. The industry has resisted bigger imports of crude when they could have been obtained easily on the international market, surpluses could have been built up, and domestic reserves could have been conserved.

We are now turning over our military oil reserves to help remedy the deficiency; so much for national security. The answer does not lie in an impossible economic self-sufficiency, but in developing a network of multilateral agreements which will provide us with alternative sources of supply, and which can be obtained by negotiations involving trade-offs beyond petroleum.

. . .

Central to the whole problem has been the explosion of private automobile traffic. There is abundant evidence that the American people did not really want the gas-guzzlers, but had a snow-job done on them by the advertisers and by the refusal of the companies to offer alternative models.

There are plenty of cars on the road these days which give 20 miles or more to the gallon. They are easy to make, if the will to do so be present. The changeover in plant, patterns, machine-tools, and processes could be completed in a year, but it seems we must wait another decade.

A revolution in energy policy, then, is required, and the main blessing of the fuel crisis is that we are being forced as a nation to do something. The elements of the solution include among other things the following:

1. A rapid shift to solar energy to pick up a substantial part, not all, of the load
2. A substantial return to coal for the time being, and temporarily to natural gas, but subject to severe environmental and mine-safety restrictions, and the ultimate need to reduce chemical combustion in terms of carbon dioxide
3. The imposition of severe environmental standards on the automobile and oil industries, so that production and distribution can be carried on without grave ecological damage
4. The phasing out of the private car from the congested areas of the big cities, and the substitution of clean, comfortable, spacious, and reasonably speedy public transit
5. The revision of national transportation policy to favor a much enlarged and publicly managed railroad network, with reduced emphasis on high-energy modes, air and highway transportation
6. The inversion of utility rate schedules to impose increasing costs on the larger consumers, with lower prices for the smaller customers
7. A shift to land irrigation systems as contrasted with high-energy chemical methods, for the tertiary treatment of municipal waste water
8. A no-nonsense, solid-waste recycling program to conserve production energy and raw materials and cut down on the rubbish

9. A shift from plastics and synthetics, which use petroleum as a raw material with high production energy demands and much pollution, to products made from natural substances

10. A changeover from chemical pesticides, with high-fossil-fuel materials requirements, to organic and integrated pest control as rapidly as possible for both ecological and economic reasons

11. Composting of sewage sludge, using garbage for the production of organic fertilizer, as contrasted with high-energy incineration accompanied by atmospheric pollution, bringing about a reduction in fossil-fuel-based, high-production-energy, high-pollution chemical fertilizers

12. The progressive elimination of those other energy guzzlers, the centrally overheated, overcooled, hermetically air-conditioned office and apartment buildings, with their artificially lighted and ventilated underground parking facilities

13. The development of land-use and industrial plant-size and location policies adapted to the reduction of daily and weekend commuting in favor of stable communities

14. Reorganization of the federal-industrial budget, reducing expenditures on big roads, big dams, and, as international agreement permits, armaments, and on misdirected research and development, in favor of socially and ecologically sound public-private investment

15. In all probability a fundamental revision of the mass-production, mass-distribution, industrial structure to reduce the one-way dumping of containers and the cross-hauling of raw materials and products.

The alternative sources of energy other than sun-power are not promising. Nuclear fission, breeders or nonbreeders, will bring a low-level but pervasive radioactive pollution from stacks and outfalls, constant workplace perils, grave danger of meltdowns, and an intolerable burden of long-lived radioactive wastes. We are well down the nuclear road without having faced these perils; it is time to slow down and back away. Nuclear fusion eludes us, and if harnessed may bring unacceptable regional thermal pollution.

Combustion plants generally, whether oil, coal, gas, or whatever, increase the carbon dioxide content of the atmosphere and could raise temperatures on the planet, disturb the global ecosystem unpredictably, and eventually precipitate the melting of the polar icecaps.

The extraction of oil from shale will be enormously costly in both ecological and economic terms. Geothermal, tidal, and wind energy may be useful, but hardly conclusive.

Obviously, the conservation of energy is imperative. The rationing of gasoline or a sharp increase in prices, or both, to meet a situation which will not be temporary, but will be permanent, in respect to oil, coupled with the strict enforcement of air pollution controls, will reduce private automobile traffic drastically and rapidly. Among the favorable consequences will be a decline in highway fatalities, in expenditures on highways, in air pollution, in hospital admissions resulting from smog, in death and incapacity from respiratory ills, including emphysema and lung cancer, and in urban sprawl. Attention can be focused again on the rebuilding of the deserted central cities within patterns of residential and workplace proximity, perhaps even of neighborhood coherence. At least as the population explosion slows down, there may be space for gracious living in the cities.

Our troubles with the Mideast about oil are indicative, not episodic. We have used up our low-cost iron ore to make autos and cans which now lie rusting in the midden heaps of the big cities or scattered over the countryside. We have stripped our old-growth forests and are placing impossible burdens on the young forests and the life they shelter. We have been drawing on the wealth of the entire globe for raw materials far out of proportion to our population. Resistance to this exploitation will take the form of raw materials embargoes and skyrocketing prices.

We shall be paying the bill for the present in greatly expanded food exports, with grave repercussions on domestic soil conservation; in water pollution from excess fertilizers, herbicides, and pesticides; and in timber exports while our paper and construction industries remain in short supply.

It may well be that the young people of America have set the best example and offer the basic solution for everyone: voluntary population stabilization. This trend must be encouraged worldwide.

But in any case, a new competence and sense of responsibility must be brought to bear swiftly on the management of our economic affairs. The public measures and institutions necessary for this purpose must now be created by the vigorous use of our democratic governmental processes. The economy must be fitted to the needs of the people.

4

The Aftermath of the Oil Crisis

The oil embargo that began in October 1973 ended in March 1974, less with a bang than with a whimper. The leading member of OPEC, Saudi Arabia, had an interest in ending the embargo, since the United States was the largest oil-consuming market in the world and the two countries had sustained close diplomatic relations since Aramco began operations in the 1940s. But Saudi Arabia and the other Arab members of OPEC would not end the embargo without assurances that Israel would return certain territory to Egypt and Syria. Secretary of State Henry Kissinger spent much of the fall and winter performing "shuttle diplomacy" between Israel and its Arab neighbors. On March 18, 1974, the Arab members of OPEC voted to end the embargo, although Syria and Libya dissented.

With the end of the embargo, Americans felt some relief that the country would have continued access to Persian Gulf oil. But high prices and the prospect of a new economic order in which OPEC would continue to exercise its control remained as vestiges of the crisis. While political leaders in Washington argued over and hammered out legislation and policies to address the "energy problem" (some still viewed it as a "crisis"), an outpouring of commentary appeared in print.

Two things stand out about this commentary. First, nearly all writers on the subject recognized that the oil embargo and OPEC's price hike were critically important events in postwar America, because these actions directly challenged U.S. power by hitting the nation in its weakest spot: its increasing reliance on imported oil. That recognition in and of itself was important, especially at a time when inflation and unemployment were on the rise. Having withdrawn without victory from its long and tragic engagement in the Vietnam War, and now in the midst of the worst presidential scandal in the nation's history, the United States was in a weakened position on the world stage.

Many people believed that America's growing dependence on foreign oil might be its true Achilles' heel if the country did not somehow develop a radical reorientation in regard to its energy needs—and the politics of those needs.

Second, whereas the embargo itself had tended to produce mostly stunned responses—it wasn't called the "oil shock" for nothing—in the aftermath of the embargo, a wide range of opinions emerged about what America should do. Environmentalists continued to maintain that the country needed to embark immediately on well-funded programs to develop renewable sources of energy and lobbied Congress to put such programs in place. In contrast, a much more belligerent attitude toward the problem developed, as is evidenced by a 1975 magazine article titled "Seizing Arab Oil" (Document 25), which advocated a military takeover of the Saudi oil fields. Between these two extremes lay many other proposals that attempted to navigate this uncharted terrain of international politics.

From 1975 to 1980, Presidents Gerald Ford and Jimmy Carter proposed many different energy programs, combining economic incentives for the domestic oil industry with conservation measures. Oil prices dipped somewhat during these years, but the 1979 Islamic revolution in Iran and the Iran-Iraq War that followed caused prices to shoot up even higher than during the crisis of 1973–1974. Both events caused severe supply disruptions, but they did not result in the same level of shock that the country had experienced in 1973–1974.

Indeed, despite supply concerns and the high price of oil in 1980, Ronald Reagan assumed the presidency with little interest in forging a government energy policy. Rather, in keeping with his conservative ideology, he believed that getting the government out of the development of energy resources would solve America's economic and political problems related to oil. Although Reagan hardly mentioned conservation, the measures taken in the 1970s—more fuel-efficient cars, better-insulated houses, and less wasteful appliances—began to pay off during his tenure. Demand did not rise as steeply as it had in the late 1960s and early 1970s, and prices steadily dropped, ultimately crashing in 1986. The members of OPEC could not agree on production controls, and the organization no longer exerted the power it had wielded during the 1970s.

24

TONY AUTH

"I Dub Thee 'Problem'"

March 11, 1974

By March 1974, after extended negotiations between Israel, its Arab neighbors, and the United States, hostilities seemed to be easing in the region. Moreover, some Arab members of OPEC, such as Saudi Arabia, were growing anxious to resume oil shipments to the United States. The Nixon administration could breathe a sigh of relief that the worst-case scenarios would not come to pass and the embargo would be lifted. At the same time, Nixon and his advisers sought to lessen national anxiety about America's future energy needs. As is evident in this cartoon, however, the energy crisis loomed large in the American consciousness.

"I dub thee 'Problem.'"

25

MILES IGNOTUS

Seizing Arab Oil

March 1975

Although Secretary of State Henry Kissinger and Defense Secretary James Schlesinger had secretly threatened to use military force to end the Arab oil embargo, the following article marked the first time that an articulation of the military options to secure oil in the Persian Gulf made it into print. This article also was unusual in that it was written under a pseudonym, Miles Ignotus — "unknown soldier" in Latin.

Who was Miles Ignotus? According to a February 4, 2004, article by Andrew Higgins in the Wall Street Journal, *the author was Edward Luttwak, "a hawkish defense expert" who advised the Pentagon. In fact, this was not the first time that Luttwak had written publicly in a hawkish vein. In October 1973 — the month that marked the beginning of the embargo and OPEC's price hikes — Luttwak and Walter Laqueur had published an article in* Commentary, *a neoconservative journal, arguing that "a western military presence will be more effective in securing the flow of oil than political measures, which are unlikely to affect the internal situation in the oil-producing countries."* [1]

The question of the authorship of "Seizing Arab Oil," as well as the ramifications of the scenarios presented in it, largely lay dormant until the U.S. invasion of Iraq in 2003, at which point top-secret intelligence reports from 1973 were declassified. These reports confirmed that the Nixon administration had considered the possibility of invading Saudi Arabia during the embargo.

After more than a year of extraordinary passivity, the United States and the other oil-consuming nations of the West have slowly—very slowly—begun debating ways to break the oil cartel's power. So far, they have pursued a futile policy of appeasement. Instead of mounting

[1] Walter Laqueur and Edward Luttwak, "Oil," *Commentary,* 56 (October 1973): 43.

Miles Ignotus, "Seizing Arab Oil," *Harper's*, March 1975, 45–62.

an economic counteroffensive against the price-rigging of the Organization of Petroleum Exporting Countries (OPEC), the victims have talked only of accommodation. Instead of a forcible reaction to protect national interests—vital national interests—they have talked about cooperation. In response, the oil cartel has predictably raised prices again, twice.

Meanwhile, economic growth in formerly developing countries, from Brazil to Taiwan, has stopped. India and the rest of the hopelessly poor have been driven into even deeper poverty. Virtually every industrialized oil importer is in deep recession, with its threat of social instability and, in turn, political disarray. Although the price of oil is not the sole cause of these troubles, it is by far the single major factor propelling inflation, unbalancing the balance of payments, and disrupting capital markets. The policy of appeasement has failed, again.

In the 1930s the craven men of Munich displayed not only an almost complacent defeatism, but also a constant need to justify German demands. Similarly, the modern appeasers have constantly tried to justify Arab oil extortion. When OPEC members began accumulating billions of dollars in unearned reserves, we were told that this was merely fair compensation for past "exploitation"—as if men who for years had been receiving huge royalties (for a product they had neither made nor found) could be said to have been exploited. When OPEC prices brought worldwide economic growth to an end, it was said that growth had been too rapid in any case—as if we had any other way to relieve poverty, and as if the military dictators and megalomaniac kings of OPEC had been chosen to oversee the ecological balance of the planet.

Many Western intellectuals have put forward an even sillier equation: OPEC = Third World = Good. To be sure, the oil cartel is bringing about a massive redistribution of the world's wealth, but it is a rather peculiar redistribution: Indian peasants buying kerosene are subsidizing the super-rich, while Americans are buying smaller cars because sheiks want bigger jets. . . .

If at last we resolve that OPEC must be broken, the question remains: how? The nonviolent methods have been discussed so much that mere mention suffices:

—*Financial denial*: Western nations in solidarity refuse OPEC deposits unless they are long-term, evenly distributed, and at low interest—or possibly under any circumstances.

—*Ownership denial*: OPEC money is forced to remain paper money since no transfer of real assets is allowed.

—*Market manipulation*: Conservation and substitution are used to cut the demand for oil, thus depressing prices once a surplus develops.

Some of these nonviolent strategies are more plausible than others, but all would in fact be utterly ineffectual. As long as OPEC controls oil supply, it will prevail: it can deny supply in the face of financial denial; withhold supply so long as purchases of Western real estate and industry are forbidden; and cut supply pro rata to offset any contrived decline in demand. As the Saudi oil minister has already explained: "If you cut demand hoping to depress prices, we will cut supply even more so as to raise prices still further." In theory again, we could cut demand to the point where the market share of OPEC producers who do need the cash is affected. To do this we must cut demand by more than the low-population, cash-surplus OPEC producers can cut supply; by the time that demand level is reached, half our industry will be without fuel, and half our work force unemployed. Nor is there any hope that enough "new" oil will be found to solve the supply problem. The funds in the North Sea, Alaska, offshore Vietnam, offshore China, and the promising structures being explored elsewhere are all useful. But their combined output—when fully developed—will not amount to half of Saudi Arabia's. And this assumes high rates of output: when it comes to reserves, all the oil found worldwide since 1965 is equivalent to a tenth of the Saudi reserves already fully proven. Even if vast new oil fields were found, it would still take five to seven years to bring them into production— and there is absolutely no reason to expect major new discoveries.

The fallacy of all the nonviolent strategies is fundamental: to break OPEC by economic means, we must break its power to control supply—and this power can always defeat the strategies first. Moreover, there are some minor practical difficulties. For the financial strategy: the Swiss would never play, but would instead launder all the money that OPEC would ever want to deposit. For the ownership-denial strategy: Japan and the gold market would never play, while OPEC investors might just want to buy all the gold in the world, plus every Japanese factory and scenic inn. Finally, for the market-manipulation strategy: for every producer willing to sell a few cargoes under the table, there is likely to be a consumer willing to buy two, in order to keep the factories running and the workers off the streets.

The Use of War

There remains only force. The only feasible countervailing power to OPEC's control of oil is power itself—military power. But the lack of any other alternative does not, of course, mean that the use of force is ipso facto feasible. First, the essential question: could we start a war on OPEC just because the price of oil is too high? Surely the answer is no. And it would probably remain so even if OPEC raises prices again, citing the rising prices of caviar, Cadillacs, and fighter-bombers.

That, however, is not the end of the story. Fortunately for us, while all members of OPEC are extortionists, some (the Arabs), are also blackmailers. Sooner or later, their demands on Israel will become excessive; the Israelis will then refuse to concede further territory without reciprocal concessions. Then there will be war, and then, at whatever cost, the Israelis will prevail again. The last Arab-Israeli war ended with the Arab armies in disarray and both Cairo and Damascus in danger. The next war is likely to end with the same result, but sooner. This time, the massive surprise of October 1973 cannot possibly be repeated, and the contest in the air will no longer feature a pre-Vietnam Israeli air force with dumb bombs and few electronic countermeasures facing post-Vietnam Arab air defenses. The Arabs may have more and better missiles, but the Israelis now have smart bombs. With Israeli fighter-bombers now making one pass instead of five or six to hit each target, Arab air defenses would have to improve by 500 to 600 percent to retain their power undiminished. Eventually the Russians will no doubt supply better guns and better missiles, but fivefold improvements would require totally new technologies, and many years to mature. Meantime, it is back to 1967 for the Israeli air force. The Arabs know this, otherwise Syrians would have opened fire in 1974. But the Israelis know this also, and they will resist Arab demands: hence war, and an embargo.

When the price problem did not exist, and Persian Gulf crude was changing hands at $1.80 per barrel or less, an Arab oil embargo was a danger to be feared, and Israel was pressured to make concessions. Now an embargo is no longer a threat but an opportunity. Some, captive to the old politics, fail to make the connection, repeating endlessly that war in the Middle East must be averted at all costs, for if Israel loses, then catastrophe, and if Israel wins, an embargo follows. There they stop. Their advice, of course, is to comply with blackmail by blackmailing Israel into further concessions. But if this dishonorable deed is done, the result will only ensure the continuation of supply at present prices, and the damage these prices are causing is altogether more fundamental than any short-term embargo could inflict. This, then, is the scenario: an Arab embargo or supply cut, an atmosphere of crisis, most probably in the aftermath of a short but bloody war. Then we go in.

The first question is where. The goal is not just to seize some oil (say, in accessible Nigeria or Venezuela) but to break OPEC. Thus force must be used selectively to occupy large and concentrated oil reserves, which can be produced rapidly in order to end the artificial scarcity of oil and thus cut the price. Faced with armed consumers occupying vast oil fields whose full output can eventually bring the price down to 50 cents per barrel, most of the producers would see virtue in agreeing to a price four or five times as high, but still six times lower than present prices. This being the ultimate goal, there is only one feasible target: Saudi Arabia. . . .

Will the world condemn America? Some of it will, and will mean it. Others, including some Europeans and unfortunate Japanese, will condemn, cry, and partake of lower oil prices with a sigh of relief. Certainly the image of the Soviet Union will improve in contrast and the United States will lose "influence and prestige in the Third World." But what influence? What prestige? And what would the spectacle of American acquiescence in the political blackmail of the kings and dictators of Araby do to American prestige? The weak respect power more than do the strong, who know its limitations.

The crucial factor, however, is domestic opinion. First, there is the why in the *raison d'état*. The American people instinctively felt that in Indochina the national interest was not at stake and only the commitment itself made for further commitment. Not so here. All would understand, all those affected by inflation and unemployment, that is.

Second, performance. All agree that had the U.S. done well *militarily* in Vietnam, public opposition would have been limited to the tiny minority of those who oppose war, or their own country, in all circumstances. The first group is certainly entitled to its elevated conceptions, but the vast majority of the people think otherwise. A neat and rapid operation *is* possible in Saudi Arabia owing to the terrain and the men, mostly absent. Moreover, the four required divisions are fit, trained, well-equipped, and battle-ready. On that score we need have no anxieties.

Third, duration. Americans were wearied by a war that was not only unsuccessful but also far too long. This operation will not be over in a day. It will last for years, though surely not until the last drop of Saudi oil is exhausted. Instead, the American-controlled distribution office of the [International Oil and Aid Organization] would allocate oil to consumers at the new low prices, but demand that they finance serious substitution efforts with some appropriate share of the vast savings on cheaper oil. Given rigid controls, diplomatic pressure, and their own caution, strong substitution policies are sure to follow in Europe, Japan, and wherever possible. And it is much easier to build nuclear power stations, hot rock generators, solar arrays, and windmills when the balance of payments is no longer in deficit, inflation has been curbed, and recession a memory—all of which $2 oil could ensure.

Hence an occupation of ten years and probably much less would suffice. Once the dust of the invasion settled, once every evidence of *permanent* intent became apparent, the remaining members of OPEC would see reason, and accept a binding commitment to maintain supplies at agreed prices in exchange for American withdrawal. From their point of view, the great danger is that Saudi oil could be used to bring the price down not to $2 but to $1.50, then $1.40, then $1.30 . . . and so on.

In a sober assessment, mindful of all the political costs and all the strategic risks, it can be done. It must be done. For if we do not do it, Project Independence will in fact be Project Isolation, with a somewhat impoverished America surrounded by a world turned into a slum. Almost everywhere, this would be an authoritarian slum, the product of utter hopelessness among the poor and mass unemployment among the former rich, all of us being forced to finance the executive jets of the sheiks and the fighter-bombers of the dictators.

If we will not do it, future generations will see through our protestations of moral restraint and recognize craven passivity. Many of those who took the United States into the jungles of Vietnam to look for the national interest are now saying that we need not do it, since we can comply with political blackmail (by blackmailing Israel in turn), and since we can afford to pay the economic extortion. True, we can do both. But the price—moral, political, and social—would be far too high. We would no longer be able to look each other in the face. Many who saw prudence and reason in bombing an ally of the Soviet Union and even blockading its ports are now saying that we cannot do it, for behind the Arabs stand the Russians, and the Russians would not let us. That, it has been argued, is false. And since no one denies that the dependence of the Western world on Arab oil is absolute, if *their* analysis were correct, it would mean that we are living at the mercy of the

Arabs, that is to say, as Prof. Robert W. Tucker has pointed out,[2] of the Russians. And if *that* is true, we no longer need a foreign policy establishment, and we might as well disband the armed forces unless we double or triple the strength: there is no sense in paying $85 billion a year for impotence.

[2]*Robert W. Tucker:* Professor of international studies and Russian studies at Princeton University, [Ed.]

26

ZUHAYR MIKDASHI

The OPEC Process

1976

Of all the people and organizations involved in the oil crisis, OPEC was perhaps the least understood, certainly by those who were not experts on international oil policy. But even among many scholarly analyses, one senses a kind of bewilderment at the power that OPEC achieved so relatively quickly. In the essay excerpted here, Zuhayr Mikdashi examined OPEC's evolution much more sympathetically. Although he evaluated both OPEC's achievements and its mistakes, he found the significance of the oil crisis in the way that OPEC redrew the balance between Western nations and the developing countries whose resources the West consumed.

Beginning in the nineteen-sixties, the spectacular growth of oil as a major source of energy in industrial societies after World War II, the emergence of developing countries as major oil exporters, and the rise of national consciousness in these countries had alerted them to the opportunities for collective action. To several of them, the conditions obtaining in the nineteen-seventies represented an opportunity to take advantage of these factors and to achieve higher levels of socio-economic development. They perceived their best strategy to be

Zuhayr Mikdashi, "The OPEC Process," in *The Oil Crisis*, ed. Raymond Vernon (New York: W. W. Norton, 1976), 214.

in the maximizing of oil receipts over a period of time that would be sufficient to permit the speedy implementation of their development programs. To these practical considerations, one should add the psychological one of "emancipation." As eloquently phrased by a former American lawmaker [Senator J. William Fulbright], "United in OPEC, they set out to redress the imbalance between cheap oil and costly imports, and also, in the psychological sense, to redress centuries of colonialism and exploitation."

The leaders of the rich industrial countries were—and remain— generally reluctant to adjust economically and psychologically to this changed balance in the division of wealth accruing from the oil trade. Some even toyed with the idea of military occupation of oil fields in order to restore the status quo. On the basis of the dramatic changes of 1973–74, one should view with some skepticism the prospect that the richer nations will willingly share their wealth and power with the less fortunate members of the international community.

OPEC might well be seen in retrospect to have been a key contributor to the changing of the character of the international system, and as a catalyst in the formation of new political relations both among nations and between nations and major "transnational" enterprises. It has already had its influence both as a protagonist in the international system and as a model to be emulated by other resource-rich underdeveloped countries. The remarkable fact about OPEC is that it proved to be a reasonably effective force for arriving at consensus, narrowing the differences in policies among member governments, and contributing to collective action.

The emergence of the importance of the OPEC national oil companies appears to be a development for the future. While the OPEC organization was dominated until the early seventies by civil servants, whose concern was to negotiate for larger governmental income from foreign concessionaire companies, by the mid-seventies, these companies had moved in to take a greater share in OPEC's decision-making processes with the objectives of seeking profitability and growth, acquiring modern technology and managerial capacity, increasing international markets, and stabilizing business relations with the outside, including the major foreign oil enterprises. By mid-1975, some OPEC national oil companies had already entered into joint ventures with the major oil companies; for example, the National Iranian Oil Company was exploring for oil in the British sector of the North Sea in cooperation with British Petroleum and was linking up with American and European enterprises in their domestic markets. Clearly, their attitude is no longer one of helpless domination by the economic enterprises of the Western world.

27

JIMMY CARTER

Two Responses to the Energy Crisis

April 1977 and January 1980

President Jimmy Carter was not the first president to call for personal sacrifice while the nation was experiencing grave energy problems. In fact, the previous president, Gerald Ford, had explicitly made such a call. But Carter was the first president to talk about America's energy consumption patterns on such a grand scale.

The Energy Problem: Address to the Nation

April 18, 1977

Two months before President Carter delivered the nationwide address excerpted here, he had appeared in a cardigan sweater before the American public to talk about energy problems and the need for people to turn their thermostats down. In this address, which previewed the National Energy Plan he would present to Congress a few days later, he did several unprecedented things. First, he gave his audience some historical detail about how the United States had arrived at the point of fearing oil embargoes. Second, he stated an array of principles that would guide his administration's work in forming an energy policy, leading off with the need for sacrifice, a commitment to economic growth, and support for protecting the environment. Throughout the address, he emphasized the difficulties that lay ahead in language that had a warlike ring to it.

Jimmy Carter, "The Energy Problem: Address to the Nation," April 18, 1977, http://www.presidency.ucsb.edu/ws/index.php?pid=7369&st=&st1=.

Good evening.

Tonight I want to have an unpleasant talk with you about a problem that is unprecedented in our history. With the exception of preventing war, this is the greatest challenge that our country will face during our lifetime.

The energy crisis has not yet overwhelmed us, but it will if we do not act quickly. It's a problem that we will not be able to solve in the next few years, and it's likely to get progressively worse through the rest of this century.

We must not be selfish or timid if we hope to have a decent world for our children and our grandchildren. We simply must balance our demand for energy with our rapidly shrinking resources. By acting now we can control our future instead of letting the future control us.

Two days from now, I will present to the Congress my energy proposals. Its Members will be my partners, and they have already given me a great deal of valuable advice.

Many of these proposals will be unpopular. Some will cause you to put up with inconveniences and to make sacrifices. The most important thing about these proposals is that the alternative may be a national catastrophe. Further delay can affect our strength and our power as a nation.

Our decision about energy will test the character of the American people and the ability of the President and the Congress to govern this Nation. This difficult effort will be the "moral equivalent of war," except that we will be uniting our efforts to build and not to destroy.

Now, I know that some of you may doubt that we face real energy shortages. The 1973 gas lines are gone, and with this springtime weather, our homes are warm again. But our energy problem is worse tonight than it was in 1973 or a few weeks ago in the dead of winter. It's worse because more waste has occurred and more time has passed by without our planning for the future. And it will get worse every day until we act.

The oil and natural gas that we rely on for 75 percent of our energy are simply running out. In spite of increased effort, domestic production has been dropping steadily at about 6 percent a year. Imports have doubled in the last 5 years. Our Nation's economic and political independence is becoming increasingly vulnerable. Unless profound changes are made to lower oil consumption, we now believe that early in the 1980s the world will be demanding more oil than it can produce.

The world now uses about 60 million barrels of oil a day, and demand increases each year about 5 percent. This means that just to stay even we need the production of a new Texas every year, an Alaskan North Slope every 9 months, or a new Saudi Arabia every 3 years. Obviously, this cannot continue. . . .

If we fail to act soon, we will face an economic, social, and political crisis that will threaten our free institutions. But we still have another choice. We can begin to prepare right now. We can decide to act while there is still time. That is the concept of the energy policy that we will present on Wednesday.

Our national energy plan is based on 10 fundamental principles. The first principle is that we can have an effective and comprehensive energy policy only if the Government takes responsibility for it and if the people understand the seriousness of the challenge and are willing to make sacrifices.

The second principle is that healthy economic growth must continue. Only by saving energy can we maintain our standard of living and keep our people at work. An effective conservation program will create hundreds of thousands of new jobs.

The third principle is that we must protect the environment. Our energy problems have the same cause as our environmental problems — wasteful use of resources. Conservation helps us solve both problems at once.

The fourth principle is that we must reduce our vulnerability to potentially devastating embargoes. We can protect ourselves from uncertain supplies by reducing our demand for oil, by making the most of our abundant resources such as coal, and by developing a strategic petroleum reserve.

The fifth principle is that we must be fair. Our solutions must ask equal sacrifices from every region, every class of people, and every interest group. Industry will have to do its part to conserve just as consumers will. The energy producers deserve fair treatment, but we will not let the oil companies profiteer.

The sixth principle, and the cornerstone of our policy, is to reduce demand through conservation. Our emphasis on conservation is a clear difference between this plan and others which merely encouraged crash production efforts. Conservation is the quickest, cheapest, most practical source of energy. Conservation is the only way that we can buy a barrel of oil for about $2. It costs about $13 to waste it.

The seventh principle is that prices should generally reflect the true replacement cost of energy. We are only cheating ourselves if we make energy artificially cheap and use more than we can really afford.

The eighth principle is that Government policies must be predictable and certain. Both consumers and producers need policies they can count on so they can plan ahead. This is one reason that I'm working with the Congress to create a new Department of Energy to replace more than 50 different agencies that now have some control over energy.

The ninth principle is that we must conserve the fuels that are scarcest and make the most of those that are plentiful. We can't continue to use oil and gas for 75 percent of our consumption, as we do now, when they only make up 7 percent of our domestic reserves. We need to shift to plentiful coal, while taking care to protect the environment, and to apply stricter safety standards to nuclear energy.

The tenth and last principle is that we must start now to develop the new, unconventional sources of energy that we will rely on in the next century. . . .

We can be sure that all the special interest groups in the country will attack the part of this plan that affects them directly. They will say that sacrifice is fine as long as other people do it, but that their sacrifice is unreasonable or unfair or harmful to the country. If they succeed with this approach, then the burden on the ordinary citizen, who is not organized into an interest group, would be crushing.

There should be only one test for this program—whether it will help our country. Other generations of Americans have faced and mastered great challenges. I have faith that meeting this challenge will make our own lives even richer. If you will join me so that we can work together with patriotism and courage, we will again prove that our great Nation can lead the world into an age of peace, independence, and freedom.

Thank you very much, and good night.

The Carter Doctrine: State of the Union Address
January 23, 1980

President Carter's attempts to craft a national energy policy fell victim to a variety of forces: interest-group wangling, legislative gridlock, Carter's own fatigue with the issue, and a new problem: the Iran hostage crisis of 1979. After an Islamic revolution in Iran that year, Iranian militants seized American hostages at the American embassy on November 4.

Jimmy Carter, "State of the Union Address," January 23, 1980, http://www.presidency.ucsb.edu/ws/index.php?pid=33079.

Fifty-two of them were retained, as hopes for a quick release evaporated during the days and weeks that followed. The regime change also resulted in a sharp drop in Iranian oil production, which in turn caused world oil prices to skyrocket and produced the decade's second oil shock in America. Gas lines returned, but the American public was in a much less introspective mood than in 1973–1974. At the highest levels of government, the combination of spiking prices and the inability of the president to secure the hostages' release sealed Carter's political fate. It also reoriented his ideas about energy. Although he still believed that Americans should curb their prodigious appetite for oil, he eventually articulated a much more aggressive stance internationally, especially following the Soviet invasion of Afghanistan in December 1979.

In Carter's second-to-last State of the Union address in January 1980, he declared that the United States would use "military force" if necessary to protect its national interest in Persian Gulf oil. The following excerpt from his address, which explained this new geopolitical policy, became known as the Carter Doctrine and has been a fundamental tenet of all subsequent presidents.

This last few months has not been an easy time for any of us. As we meet tonight, it has never been more clear that the state of our Union depends on the state of the world. And tonight, as throughout our own generation, freedom and peace in the world depend on the state of our Union.

The 1980s have been born in turmoil, strife, and change. This is a time of challenge to our interests and our values and it's a time that tests our wisdom and our skills. . . .

We superpowers . . . have the responsibility to exercise restraint in the use of our great military force. The integrity and the independence of weaker nations must not be threatened. They must know that in our presence they are secure.

. . . The Soviet Union has taken a radical and an aggressive new step. It's using its great military power against a relatively defenseless nation. The implications of the Soviet invasion of Afghanistan could pose the most serious threat to the peace since the Second World War. . . .

The region which is now threatened by Soviet troops in Afghanistan is of great strategic importance: It contains more than two-thirds of the world's exportable oil. The Soviet effort to dominate Afghanistan has brought Soviet military forces to within 300 miles of the Indian Ocean and close to the Strait of Hormuz, a waterway through which most of the world's oil must flow. The Soviet Union is now attempting to consolidate a strategic position, therefore, that poses a grave threat to the free movement of Middle East oil.

This situation demands careful thought, steady nerves, and resolute action, not only for this year but for many years to come. It demands collective efforts to meet this new threat to security in the Persian Gulf and in Southwest Asia. It demands the participation of all those who rely on oil from the Middle East and who are concerned with global peace and stability. And it demands consultation and close cooperation with countries in the area which might be threatened.

Meeting this challenge will take national will, diplomatic and political wisdom, economic sacrifice, and, of course, military capability. We must call on the best that is in us to preserve the security of this crucial region.

Let our position be absolutely clear: An attempt by any outside force to gain control of the Persian Gulf region will be regarded as an assault on the vital interests of the United States of America, and such an assault will be repelled by any means necessary, including military force.

28

REPUBLICAN PARTY PLATFORM

Position on Energy

July 15, 1980

Over the course of the twentieth century, political party platforms hammered out during presidential nominating conventions became more and more loquacious and detailed. The products of intense negotiation among interest groups, politicians, and party operatives, platforms are typically ignored by the average voter, but they nonetheless represent a window on shifting patterns in partisan politics. In the following excerpt from the Republican party platform in 1980, the party was clearly trying

"Republican Party Platform of 1980," July 15, 1980, http://www.presidency.ucsb.edu /showplatforms.php?platindex=R1980.

to differentiate its position on energy from what was characterized as
Carter's "pessimistic attitude" toward America's energy future.

Energy is the lifeblood of our economy. Without adequate energy supplies now and in the future, the jobs of American men and women, the security of their lives, and their ability to provide for their families will be threatened and their standard of living will be lowered. Every American is painfully aware that our national energy situation has deteriorated badly over the past four years of Democratic control. Gasoline prices have more than doubled. Our oil import bill has risen 96 percent. Our energy supplies have become increasingly vulnerable because U.S. oil production outside of Alaska is now 28 percent below 1973 levels. The threat of sudden shortages, curtailments, and gas lines has become a recurring reality.

This steady deterioration has not only compounded our economic problems of inflation, recession, and dollar weakness, but even more importantly, it has infected our confidence as a nation. Energy shortages, spiralling costs, and increasing insecurity are beginning to darken our basic hopes and expectations for the future.

The National Association for the Advancement of Colored People has very accurately focused on the effects that a no-growth energy policy will have on the opportunities of America's black people and other minorities. The NAACP said that "a pessimistic attitude toward energy supplies for the future . . . cannot satisfy the fundamental requirement of a society of expanding economic opportunity."

In commenting on the Carter energy proposals, the Association said, "We cannot accept the notion that our people are best served by a policy based upon the inevitability of energy shortage and the need for government to allocate an ever diminishing supply among competing interests. . . . [The plan] reflects the absence of a black perspective in its development."

Three and one-half years ago, President Carter declared energy the "moral equivalent of war" and sent Congress 109 recommendations for action, including the creation of a new Department of Energy. Since then, the federal budget for government's energy bureaucracy has grown to about $10 billion per year and more than 20,000 pages of new energy regulations and guidelines have been issued. But these have not fostered the production of a single extra unit of energy.

The Democratic Congress has joined in the stampede, taking action on 304 energy bills since 1977. As a result, the federal bureaucracy is

busy from coast to coast allocating gasoline, setting building temperatures, printing rationing coupons, and readying standby plans to ban
weekend boating, close factories, and pass out "no drive day" stickers
to American motorists—all the time saying, "We must make do with
less." Never before in the history of American government has so
much been done at such great expense with such dismal results.

Republicans believe this disappointing cycle of shrinking energy
prospects and expanding government regulation and meddling is
wholly unnecessary. We believe that the proven American values of
individual enterprise can solve our energy problems. This optimism
stands in stark contrast to the grim predictions of the Democrats who
have controlled Congress for the last 25 years. . . .

We believe the United States must proceed on a steady and orderly
path toward energy self-sufficiency. But in the interim, our pressing
need for insurance against supply disruption should not be made
hostage to the whims of foreign governments, as is presently the case
under the Carter Administration.

29

RONALD REAGAN

National Energy Policy Plan
July 17, 1981

*President Ronald Reagan brought a new perspective to America's energy
problem. He conceived of it as a problem with the government's response
to the oil crisis, not as a problem with energy itself. In this brief message
to Congress, which accompanied his administration's submission of its
National Energy Policy Plan in July 1981, Reagan stated succinctly his
belief that the market alone would take care of America's energy needs.
Noting that his plan represented a "break" with the past, Reagan expressed his optimism that removing government interventions in the
economy would advance individuals' and the nation's welfare.*

Ronald Reagan, "Message to the Congress Transmitting the National Energy Policy Plan,"
July 17, 1981, http://www.presidency.ucsb.edu/ws/index.php?pid=44096&st=&st1=.

To the Congress of the United States:

The National Energy Policy Plan that I am sending you, as required by Section 801 of the Department of Energy Organization Act (Public Law 95-91), represents a break from the format and philosophy of the two National Energy Plans that preceded it.

Our national energy plan should not be a rigid set of production and conservation goals dictated by Government. Our primary objective is simply for our citizens to have enough energy, and it is up to them to decide how much energy that is, and in what form and manner it will reach them. When the free market is permitted to work the way it should, millions of individual choices and judgments will produce the proper balance of supply and demand our economy needs.

Overall, the outlook for this country's energy supplies is not nearly as grim as some have painted it, although our problems are not all behind us. The detailed projections, along with the supplementary documents on environmental and economic questions, are being submitted separately by the Secretary of Energy.

The approach explained in the basic National Energy Policy Plan cannot be divorced from the Administration's program for national economic recovery. Energy is one important aspect of our society, but it is only one.

This Administration's actions to end oil price controls and to dismantle the cumbersome regulatory apparatus associated with those controls demonstrate the intent stated in my February 18 economic message to minimize Federal intervention in the marketplace. Reforms in leasing policies and the removal of unnecessary environmental restrictions upon the production, delivery, and use of energy are part of this same effort to reduce bureaucratic burdens on all Americans.

This does not mean that the Federal government is withdrawing from all involvement in energy. It cannot and should not. The Government itself is directly responsible for lands which contain a major share of our resource wealth.

There is also an appropriate Federal role in certain long-term research and development related to energy production and distribution. The goal of these projects is to develop promising technological innovations to the point where private enterprise can reasonably assess their risks.

Given our continued vulnerability to energy supply disruptions, certain emergency preparations—such as rapid filling of the Strategic Petroleum Reserve—remain principally a Government responsibility.

But our basic role is to provide a sound and stable economic and policy environment that will enable our citizens, businesses, and governmental units at all levels to make rational decisions on energy use and production—decisions that reflect the true value, in every sense, of all the Nation's resources.

5

The Legacy of the Oil Crisis

The oil crisis of 1973–1974 slowly faded from public memory. Although the massive oil spill in Prince William Sound, Alaska, in 1989 revived the anger and anxiety that had followed the Santa Barbara blowout twenty years earlier, the desire for cheap oil overshadowed environmentalist critiques of America's petroleum-based society. In 1986, oil prices dropped precipitously and for the most part remained low for the rest of the century. Auto manufacturers responded by building larger cars, and Americans flocked to dealers in search of pricey new trucks and sport-utility vehicles (SUVs) that did not have to comply with the automobile efficiency standards set by Congress. The days when car advertisements could sing the praises of fuel efficiency were long gone.

As SUVs in particular grew more expensive and ever larger, some Americans began to complain about their dismal gas mileage and their effect on the environment. Throughout the 1990s, scientists amassed evidence that burning fossil fuels, which released carbon dioxide into the atmosphere, was primarily responsible for potentially profound changes in the planet's climate. In 1997, under the aegis of the United Nations, 160 countries reached an agreement called the Kyoto Protocol, which required each country to reduce emissions of greenhouse gases by a certain percentage by 2012. Within two years, more than 150 countries had ratified the agreement. However, due to deep political opposition in the United States—and especially to President George W. Bush's opposition to the agreement, which he declared early in his first administration—the U.S. Senate did not ratify the protocol.

While Americans were gassing up their cars with nonchalance during the 1990s, oil came to occupy an increasingly important place in the United States' international strategy. After the Carter Doctrine (Document 28) asserted that the U.S. government would protect its national interest in the oil reserves of the Persian Gulf, the United States increased its military presence in the region. In 1983, Ronald Reagan established the United States Central Command (CENTCOM) to oversee

134

America's security interests in the Persian Gulf. When Saddam Hussein invaded Kuwait in August 1990—in large part to gain control of that country's oil production following Iraq's devastating ten-year war with Iran—the United States responded by sending in troops. The resulting Persian Gulf War in 1991 quickly freed Kuwait from Iraqi occupation, established international sanctions against Iraq and particularly its oil industry, and showed the United States' overwhelming military force. "By God, we've kicked the Vietnam syndrome," President George Herbert Walker Bush proclaimed at the war's swift end, indicating that the nation's successful use of military power would give it renewed confidence to handle international conflicts in the future.

That confidence reigned supreme throughout the 1990s as the United States' growing economy was once again the envy of the world. With the collapse of communism and the fall of the Soviet Union in 1989–1991, no other nation could compete with America internationally. But by 2000, the stock market was beginning to weaken, and the economy began to slow down. Then, on September 11, 2001, Al Qaeda's attack on the World Trade Center and the Pentagon transformed America's domestic and international politics. The nation's relationship with the Middle East took center stage, as the United States waged war on Afghanistan (2001) and Iraq (2003), and concerns about oil prices and supplies reentered the political arena. Suddenly, the oil crisis of 1973–1974 was no longer just a distant memory.

30

BILL McKIBBEN

The Climate Crisis

1989

In 1989, the year the Exxon Valdez *supertanker spilled 11 million gallons of oil into Prince William Sound, Alaska, writer Bill McKibben published* The End of Nature, *a controversial book about the prospects of global warming. McKibben argued that because humans had caused the*

Bill McKibben, From *The End of Nature* (New York: Anchor Books, 1989; Rept. ed., 1997), 10–11, 18–19.

earth's warming—through burning fossil fuels that released carbon dioxide, the main component of greenhouse gases—there was now no place on earth where one could experience nature as separate from human influence. His book, excerpted here, sparked tremendous debate, especially over the science behind climate change, and many people disputed that human causes had anything at all to do with global warming.

Over the years, scientists embraced the idea of "climate change" rather than "global warming," as they understood that the earth's warming would create a vast range of complex transformations around the planet, such as a rise in sea level (due to melting arctic ice sheets) and the potential for increasingly severe Atlantic Ocean hurricanes. Since the 1990s, climate change science has continued to paint an unsettling picture of what is to come. Especially disturbing is the speed of that change, as scientists now understand it. Whereas most climate scientists and environmentalists in the late 1980s and early 1990s imagined that global warming would happen at a deliberate pace, increasing evidence shows that climate change is accelerating, particularly in the arctic regions, where warming trends have been accentuated. Although many critics at the time thought that McKibben's book was an exercise in apocalypticism, the years since have confirmed that human-caused climate change will be the major environmental challenge of the future.

When we drill into an oil field, we tap into a vast reservoir of organic matter that has been in storage for millennia. We unbury it. When we burn that oil (or coal or natural gas) we release its carbon into the atmosphere in the form of carbon dioxide. This is not pollution in the normal sense of the word. Carbon *monoxide* is "pollution," an unnecessary by-product. A clean-burning engine releases less of it. But when it comes to carbon dioxide, a clean-burning engine is no better than the motor on a Model T. It will emit about 5.6 pounds of carbon in the form of carbon dioxide for every gallon of gasoline it consumes. . . .

. . . We have increased the amount of carbon dioxide in the air by about 25 percent in the last century, and will almost certainly double it in the next; we have more than doubled the level of methane; we have added a soup of other gases. *We have substantially altered the earth's atmosphere.*

This is not like local pollution, not like smog over Los Angeles. This is the earth's entire atmosphere. If you'd climbed some remote mountain in 1960 and sealed up a bottle of air at its peak, and did the same thing this year, the two samples would be substantially different.

Their basic chemistry would have changed. Most discussions of the greenhouse gases rush immediately to their future consequences—is the sea going to rise?—without pausing to let the simple fact of what has already happened sink in. The air around us, even where it is clean, and smells like spring, and is filled with birds, is *different*, significantly changed.

That said, the question of what this new atmosphere means must arise. If it means nothing, we'd soon forget about it, since the air would be as colorless and odorless as before and as easy to breathe. And, indeed, the direct effects *are* unnoticeable. Anyone who lives indoors breathes carbon dioxide at a level several times the atmospheric concentration without ill effects; the federal government limits industrial workers to a chronic exposure of five thousand parts per million, or almost fifteen times the current atmospheric levels; a hundred years from now a child at recess will still breathe far less carbon dioxide than a child in a classroom.

This, however, is only mildly good news. The effects on us will be slightly less direct, but nevertheless drastic: changes in the atmosphere will change the weather, and *that* will change recess. The temperature, the rainfall, the speed of the wind will change. The chemistry of the upper atmosphere may seem an abstraction, a text written in a foreign language. But its translation into the weather of New York and Cincinnati and San Francisco will alter the lives of all of us.

31

NATIONAL SECURITY COUNCIL

Oil and National Security Interests

August 20, 1990

Eighteen days after Saddam Hussein's forces invaded Kuwait, President George H. W. Bush met with his National Security Council to decide what U.S. policy should be toward the invasion. Still committing the nation to working within diplomatic channels, Bush nonetheless emphasized

"National Security Directive 45," August 20, 1990, http://www.gwu.edu/~nsarchiv/NSAEBB/NSAEBB39/document2.pdf.

the central place that Persian Gulf oil had in America's strategic inter-
ests. As is evident in the following excerpt from a document that was
declassified in 1996, he committed U.S. forces "to deter and, if necessary,
defend Saudi Arabia and other friendly states in the Gulf region from
further Iraqi aggression."

During the autumn of 1990, as President Bush and his advisers real-
ized that diplomatic channels offered little hope for turning back Iraq's
occupation of Kuwait, they clearly leaned toward military intervention.
Not wanting to replicate America's military engagement in Vietnam,
which had occurred without a formal vote by Congress to commit troops,
Bush sought congressional support for military action. He received that
support, but only after Congress debated the legitimacy of waging a war
that would be fought, at least in part, to secure American access to Per-
sian Gulf oil.

U.S. Interests

U.S. interests in the Persian Gulf are vital to the national security.
These interests include access to oil and the security and stability of
key friendly states in the region. The United States will defend its vital
interests in the area, through the use of U.S. military force if necessary and appropriate, against any power with interests inimical to our
own. The United States also will support the individual and collective
self-defense of friendly countries in the area to enable them to play a
more active role in their own defense. The United States will encourage the effective expressions of support and the participation of our
allies and other friendly states to promote our mutual interests in the
Persian Gulf region. . . .

Energy

The United States now imports nearly half the oil it consumes and, as
a result of the current crisis, could face a major threat to its economy.
Much of the world is even more dependent on imported oil and more
vulnerable to Iraqi threats. To minimize any impact that oil flow reductions from Iraq and Kuwait will have on the world's economies, it will
be our policy to ask oil-producing nations to do what they can to
increase production to offset these losses. I also direct the Secretaries
of State and Energy to explore with the member countries of the Inter-

national Energy Agency (IEA) a coordinated drawdown of strategic petroleum reserves, and implementation of complementary measures. I will continue to ask the American public to exercise restraint in their own consumption of oil products. The Secretary of Energy should work with various sectors of the U.S. economy to encourage energy conservation and fuel switching to non-oil sources, where appropriate and economic. Finally, I will continue to appeal to oil companies to show restraint in their pricing of crude oil and products. The Secretary of Energy, as appropriate, should work with oil companies in this regard.

Military

To protect U.S. interests in the Gulf and in response to requests from the King of Saudi Arabia and the Amir of Kuwait, I have ordered U.S. military forces deployed to the region for two purposes: to deter and, if necessary, defend Saudi Arabia and other friendly states in the Gulf region from further Iraqi aggression; and to enforce the mandatory Chapter 7 sanctions under Article 51 of the UN Charter and UNSC Resolutions 660 and 661. U.S. forces will work together with those of Saudi Arabia and other Gulf countries to preserve their national integrity and to deter further Iraqi aggression. Through their presence, as well as through training and exercises, these multinational forces will enhance the overall capability of Saudi Arabia and other regional states to defend themselves.

I also approve U.S. participation, in conjunction with the forces of other friendly governments, in two separate multinational forces that would provide for the defense of Saudi Arabia and enforce the UN mandated sanctions.

32

The SUV: Master or Monster of the Road?

1999

As the century drew to a close and with a seemingly boundless economy, SUVs began to draw a great deal of public commentary, as the two documents that follow show.

JERRY EDGERTON

I Want My SUV

October 1, 1999

The high volume of SUV sales in the late 1990s clearly indicated that Americans loved these roomy and powerful vehicles. As the following document illustrates, many people felt relatively untroubled by charges that SUVs were too excessive or that they might be unsafe.

It seems like only yesterday that my 1995 Ford Explorer was brand new and the envy of friends and colleagues. But lately, when it comes to my sport utility, I find myself under attack. "Why do you really need an SUV in New York City?" ask neighbors and co-workers. They appear to think it's because I want to crush small cars, tower over taxis and reignite a gas crisis. Even the ethics columnist in the *New York Times* Sunday magazine has pronounced owning a sport utility in Manhattan immoral. When I field questions online from readers around the country, I hear the same gripes: SUVs are big, dangerous, obnoxious indulgences.

The Oct. 1 rollout of Ford's new super-size Excursion sport utility is sure to inflame these attacks. The $34,000-and-up Excursion exempli-

Jerry Edgerton, "I Want My SUV," *Money*, October 1, 1999, 140.

fies everything so many car owners love to hate about SUVs. It's the longest (nearly 19 feet), widest (six feet, eight inches) and tallest (six feet, four inches) ute[1] on the road; it averages a mere 12 miles a gallon; and, because it weighs more than 8,500 pounds when fully loaded, the Excursion isn't subject to the "light truck" pollution emission standards that cover most SUVs, pickups and minivans. Environmentalists have taken notice; the Sierra Club has dubbed it "the Ford Valdez."

I recently test-drove an Excursion and found it too big for my liking. The length and bulk make it maneuver like a recreational vehicle, especially on narrow roads. But Ford will likely find ready buyers among utility owners who tow trailers or haul a whole soccer team, many of whom now drive the largest SUV, the Chevrolet Suburban.

Even if the Excursion isn't for me, I still love SUVs. So do plenty of other drivers. The sport utility share of the new-car market has nearly doubled in the past five years to 18% of all vehicle sales. (The light-truck category—SUVs plus minivans and pickups—accounts for just under 50%.) That popularity may be driving the backlash. With more SUVs on the road, more car owners get angry when they can't see around an SUV or they find the headlights of a high-riding ute shining in their eyes.

But booming sales alone don't explain the wrath. I don't hear SUV-like anger about pickups, which account for even more new-vehicle sales—20%—and pose similar problems. My theory is that SUVs have taken their place alongside big houses as hated symbols of conspicuous consumption.

[1] *ute*: Slang for sport-utility vehicle [Ed.].

SUSAN ELLICOTT

Big Wheels

March 6, 1999

In the following document, one observer relished the charge that SUVs were excessive and wasteful, poking fun at the automobile industry's seemingly insatiable desire to manufacture gigantic vehicles.

Susan Ellicott, "Big Wheels," *New York Times*, March 6, 1999, p. A13.

The Ford Motor Company today introduced the first design changes to make the rising number of huge sport utility vehicles a little safer in crashes with cars. It said its newest sport utility vehicle, a behemoth that would be the tallest and heaviest yet, would be equipped with hollow steel bars mounted below the front and rear bumpers to prevent it from riding over cars during collisions. The horizontal steel beams hang down six inches from the high-riding steel frame of the vehicle, the Ford Excursion, which is nearly seven feet tall and weighs more than three tons.

—The *New York Times*, Feb. 27

Unconfirmed leaks in the car industry press suggest that the Excursion, an improved version of the Expedition, which itself upgraded the once popular Explorer, is a precursor to several even larger and heavier sport utility models expected within the next three years.

First off the production line will be the Extravagance. At 90 inches wide, compared with the Excursion's 80 inches, it will be the first sport model to be classified as an extra-wide vehicle and therefore required by Federal regulations to carry special running lights on the roof and sides. The Extravagance will be available in 150 colors, but not yellow, which Ford researchers rejected after studies showed that a yellow mock-up was frequently mistaken in tests for a school bus, especially when the driver's side stop sign swung out.

Auto-industry life-style researchers are said to be especially pleased with the Extravagance's beverage holder. With a capacity for up to four grande lattes, the holder will be the first to be built of flexible steel beams and to have a double layer of insulation. Company safety officials said that, in the event of a head-on collision, the holder is designed to bend and absorb energy, thereby minimizing the amount of dangerous hot spillage.

Ford intends to market an even larger model, the Exorbitance, as soon as lovers of sport utility vehicles finally lose all sense of scale, a development that car industry analysts predict will take only a few weeks once the Extravagance hits the roads.

Also on the drawing board is the Extraneous, a nine-foot sport vehicle that is actually just a Taurus attached to a four-ton steel ball. The car is said to be extremely safe, except when moving.

The Extravagance will be the first sport vehicle with an adjustable reinforced frame. Features will include a computerized driver's "eye" that will detect any impending collision and automatically expand the

Extravagance's axles to go over and/or around any obstructions, including smaller sport vehicles.

While applauding the vehicle's new safety devices, environmentalists are appalled at the Extravagance's low gas mileage—as little as five miles per gallon in the city with a V-12 engine. But the vehicle's designers argue that the impressively high gasoline consumption could actually decrease global warming by encouraging owners to set out on only essential errands. And Ford's life-style consultants say that, if sport vehicles get big enough, they may eventually eliminate the need for their owners to drive anywhere at all.

The company reportedly intends to introduce the capstone of its utility models, the Excessive, by late 2001. It is said the Excessive could measure up to 40 feet in length and weigh a staggering five tons, with room for 20 people in four rows of seats, excluding sleeping quarters, dining area, children's playroom and maid's room. Optional extras are said to include an Imax-style simulation of the trading floor of the New York Stock Exchange.

33

Testimony before Congress about Fuel Efficiency
2000 and 2001

The debate over SUVs went beyond simply what they symbolized, as environmentalists and some politicians began pushing for more stringent fuel-efficiency standards. In the documents that follow, representatives from the Sierra Club and the Alliance of Automobile Manufacturers pleaded their respective cases in congressional hearings regarding updating the Corporate Average Fuel Economy (CAFE) standards established in 1975.

DANIEL F. BECKER, SIERRA CLUB

Testimony before House Committee on Resources

April 12, 2000

In the following excerpt from hearings held by the House Committee on Resources in 2000, Sierra Club representative Daniel Becker maintained that the CAFE standards established in 1975 were effective regulatory mechanisms for protecting the environment. Moreover, he argued that in response to increasing oil prices, Congress should enact tougher CAFE standards rather than increase domestic production of oil by allowing drilling in the Arctic National Wildlife Refuge.

Mr. Chairman and Members of the Committee, my name is Daniel Becker and I am the Director of Sierra Club's Global Warming and Energy Program. I appreciate the opportunity to testify on behalf of Sierra Club's more than half million members nationwide on how we can improve our energy security and cut our oil dependency. In short we should not drill under the Arctic National Wildlife Refuge for oil. We should drill under Detroit by making our cars go further on a gallon of gas.

Once more, oil prices have risen because OPEC—a cartel of oil producing countries—is manipulating supply to increase profits. Once more, we find ourselves vulnerable and victimized by our dependence on foreign oil. And once more, Americans, tired of being jerked around by the cartel, look to their leaders for real solutions.

But instead of using the last quarter-century to reduce America's oil dependency, Congress has bowed to the oil companies and auto industry refusing to encourage American car companies to make more fuel efficient cars and voting against research and incentives for alternate energy use. Since 1995, a rider on the Transportation Appropriations bill has frozen Corporate Average Fuel Economy.

Today's high prices at the pump are the result of high demand in the face of a small shortfall in world oil supply. Globally, oil consumption is 2 million barrels of oil per day more than supply because of

Daniel F. Becker, Testimony before House Committee on Resources, *National Security and Strategies for Reducing Oil Imports*, 106th Cong., 2nd sess., April 12, 2000.

OPEC's decision to cut back on production by 4 million barrels per day. The U.S. alone consumes about 18 million barrels a day. The U.S. share of this shortfall is about 400,000 barrels per day. If, in 1994, a 6% per year increase had been phased in, CAFE standards alone would have eliminated twice the U.S. share of excess demand according to analysis by the American Council for an Energy Efficient Economy.

Now some members of Congress are using the oil price hike as an excuse to renew their calls for drilling the Arctic Refuge. Clearly, destroying one of the most spectacular places on the planet is too high a price to pay for politics as usual. . . .

To some, the solution to ending our dependence on foreign oil is simple: increase domestic supply. While close to half our oil is produced domestically, the U.S. has less than 3% of the world's known oil reserves. The numbers will never add up to oil independence. And our oil deficit is only getting worse. The U.S. currently imports 55% of its oil. At the height of the oil crisis in 1975, the U.S. imported just 35% of its oil. Within the next few years the U.S. Energy Information Agency projects that we will be importing nearly two-thirds of our oil. . . .

Oil meets 40% of our energy needs. The transportation sector is the leader in oil demand, with motor fuels accounting for 65% of oil consumption—mostly in the form of gasoline. In fact, cars and light trucks alone guzzle 40% of the oil consumed in the U.S. Demand for gasoline has been steadily rising, in large part due to the boom in light truck sales, especially sport utility vehicles. Today, about half of all new vehicles sold in America are light trucks. Many of these are SUVs, which average 12–16 [miles per gallon]. . . .

Though some say the answer to our nation's energy needs lie[s] below the surface of the Arctic National Wildlife Refuge, this spectacular landscape need not—and must not—be sacrificed for a few barrels of oil. Ninety-five percent of Alaska's vast North Slope is already available for oil and gas exploration and leasing. The coastal plain of the Arctic Refuge represents the last 5% that remains off-limits to drilling. But Big Oil wants it all.

The coastal plain of the Arctic National Wildlife Refuge is America's Serengeti. Nestled between the towering mountains of the Brooks Range and the Beaufort Sea in northeast Alaska, the narrow 1.5 million acre coastal plain is the biological heart of this untamed wilderness. It is home to unique and abundant wildlife: wolves, polar bear, musk ox and wolverine. Myriad bird species rely on the coastal plain for breeding, nesting and migratory stopovers on trips as far away as the Baja peninsula, the Chesapeake Bay, and even Antarctica. . . .

But it doesn't matter how much or how little oil may lie underneath the coastal plain. Drilling the Arctic Refuge would be as shortsighted as damming the Grand Canyon for hydroelectric power or tapping Old Faithful for geothermal energy. It would be as foolhardy as burning the *Mona Lisa* to keep you warm. America is losing our remaining wildlands at an alarming rate. We must have the foresight to protect one of America's most spectacular natural treasures—not sacrifice it for a minimal amount of oil.

JOSEPHINE S. COOPER,
ALLIANCE OF AUTOMOBILE MANUFACTURERS
Testimony before House Committee on Ways and Means
June 13, 2001

When the discussion of CAFE standards took place in Congress in 2001, within a larger discussion of America's energy resources and tax laws, President George W. Bush's administration made it clear that it preferred using tax incentives, rather than regulation, to encourage automobile manufacturers to develop and sell vehicles with better fuel economy. In this document, excerpted from testimony before the House Ways and Means Committee, the president of the Alliance of Automobile Manufacturers outlined why her membership supported the administration's policy and rejected increased regulation. Bush did enact such incentives, but as oil prices climbed precipitously in 2004 and 2005, the debate over CAFE standards continued.

Thank you for the opportunity to testify before your Subcommittee regarding energy policy issues. My name is Josephine S. Cooper and I am President and CEO of the Alliance of Automobile Manufacturers, a trade association of 13 car and light-truck manufacturers. Our member companies include BMW of North America, Inc., DaimlerChrysler Corporation, Fiat, Ford Motor Company, General Motors Corporation, Isuzu Motors of America, Mazda, Mitsubishi, Nissan North America,

Josephine S. Cooper, Testimony before House Committee on Ways and Means, *Energy and Tax Laws*, 107th Cong., 1st sess., June 13, 2001.

Porsche, Toyota Motor North America, Volkswagen of America, and Volvo.

Alliance member companies have more than 620,000 employees in the United States, with more than 250 manufacturing facilities in 35 states. Overall, a recent University of Michigan study found that the entire automobile industry creates more than 6.6 million direct and spin-off jobs in all 50 states and produces almost $243 billion in payroll compensation annually.

The Alliance supports efforts to create an effective energy policy based on broad, market-oriented principles. Policies that promote research development and deployment of advanced technologies and provide customer based incentives to accelerate demand of these advanced technologies set the foundation. This focus on bringing advanced technologies to market leverages the intense competition of the automobile manufacturers worldwide. Incentives will help consumers overcome the initial cost barriers of advanced technologies during early market introduction and increase demand, bringing more energy efficient vehicles into the marketplace.

This year, there has been increased attention on vehicles and their fuel economy levels with particular discussion of the Corporate Average Fuel Economy (CAFE) program. Rather than simply engage in an exercise updating a 26-year-old program with all of its flaws, Congress needs to consider new approaches for the 21st century. The Alliance and its 13 member companies believe that the best approach for improved fuel efficiency is to aggressively promote the development of advanced technologies—through cooperative, public/private research programs and competitive development—and incentives to help pull the technologies into the marketplace as rapidly as possible. We know that advanced technologies with the potential for major fuel economy gains are possible. As a nation, we need to get these technologies on the road as soon as possible in an effort to reach the national energy goals as fast and as efficiently as we can.

The Alliance is pleased that Vice President [Dick] Cheney's National Energy Policy report recommends and supports a tax credit for advanced technology vehicles (ATVs). Specifically, it proposes a tax credit for consumers who purchase a new hybrid or fuel cell vehicle between 2002 and 2007. In addition, the report supported the broader use of alternative fuel and alternative vehicles. This is consistent with the Alliance's position of supporting enactment of tax credits for consumers to help offset the initial higher costs of advanced technology and alternative fuel vehicles until more advancements and greater volumes make them less expensive to produce and purchase. . . .

. . . Higher standards may result in vehicles that are less attractive to customers in terms of meeting their needs for work and family. If consumer demand is not aligned with manufacturers' production, there is the potential for significant negative impact on employment throughout the industry. Ultimately, any fuel savings that result will come at high cost to consumers, manufacturers and the economy. In short, automakers need to produce vehicles that appeal to customers. CAFE acts as a market intrusion that over time will create distortions and unintended adverse consequences.

Recent sales figures support this position. The top ten most fuel-efficient vehicles account for less than 2% of total sales. The ultimate goal for any business is to provide products consumers want to buy. Increasing CAFE standards will require automakers to produce less of the products that American consumers are actually purchasing today and more of the products that are in lower demand. . . .

To reiterate, a better way to improve vehicle and fleet fuel economy, and one that is more in tune with consumer preferences, is to encourage the development and purchase of advanced technology vehicles (ATVs). Consumers are in the driver's seat and most independent surveys show that Americans place a high priority on performance, safety, space and other issues with fuel economy ranking much lower even with today's gas prices. ATVs hold great promise for increases in fuel efficiency without sacrificing the other vehicle attributes consumers desire. Just as important, the technology is transparent to the customer. . . .

These advanced technology vehicles are more expensive than their gasoline counterparts during early market introduction. As I mentioned earlier, the Alliance is supportive of Congressional legislation that would provide for personal and business end-user tax incentives for the purchase of advanced technology and alternative fuel vehicles. Make no mistake: across the board, tax credits will not completely cover the incremental costs of new advanced technology. However, [they] will make consumers more comfortable with accepting the technology and begin to change purchasing behavior. In short, tax credits will help bridge the gap towards winning broad acceptance among the public leading to greater volume and sales figures throughout the entire vehicle fleet. This type of incentive will help "jump start" market penetration and support broad energy efficiency and diversity goals.

34

NEELA BANERJEE

Saudi Oil after 9/11

October 21, 2001

The links between oil and the September 11 attacks on the United States, as well our nation's responses, are far from simple. Al Qaeda leader Osama bin Laden had long made clear his anger at the stationing of U.S. troops in Saudi Arabia during the Persian Gulf War, which had resulted in part from George H. W. Bush's fear that Saddam Hussein might consider oil supplies there fair game. Securing American access to Persian Gulf oil also contributed to George W. Bush's decision to invade Iraq in 2003. In the following article, which appeared a little over a month after the 9/11 attacks, New York Times *correspondent Neela Banerjee explored the array of potential political problems that U.S. dependence on Saudi oil had created.*

During his presidential campaign, George W. Bush warned that the nation faced an oil crisis. He was right, but not in the way he foresaw. The crisis that came has nothing to do with prices at the gas pump, or environmental obstacles to drilling in the Arctic National Wildlife Refuge in Alaska.

Rather, it has to do with the political and military price the United States must pay for its dependence on oil from the Persian Gulf.

The terms of that dependence have been glaringly obvious since the attacks on New York and Washington. Immediately after Sept. 11, the Organization of the Petroleum Exporting Countries, led by Saudi Arabia, assured the United States that it would keep oil supplies stable.

In turn, the Bush administration has refrained from criticizing Saudi silence over the American-led counterattacks against Osama bin Laden and the Taliban, nor has it spoken out about evidence that Saudi citizens finance Osama bin Laden's Al Qaeda network and other radical Islamic organizations.

Neela Banerjee, "The High, Hidden Cost of Saudi Arabian Oil," *New York Times*, October 21, 2001, p. WK3.

Moreover, although the Federal Bureau of Investigation identified most of the hijackers in the Sept. 11 attacks as Saudis, Saudi Arabia has refused to provide passenger lists of flights to the United States, an act the Bush administration has been unwilling to criticize.

"The stark truth is that we're dependent on this country that directly or indirectly finances people who are a direct threat to you and me as individuals," said Edward L. Morse, former deputy assistant secretary of state for international energy policy under President Ronald Reagan.

"They won't give us information, won't help track people down, and won't let us use our bases that are there to protect them," Mr. Morse added.

A major reason for that reticence is oil. Five percent of the world's population lives in the United States, but it burns about 19 million barrels of oil a day, or 25 percent of the global daily consumption of 76 million barrels. American cars and sport-utility vehicles alone consume 10 percent of that.

The United States has been angling for influence in the Arabian peninsula since oil was discovered there 70 years ago. American oil companies helped create Saudi Aramco, the state oil company. They were kicked out during the 1973 Arab oil embargo, but the United States and Saudi Arabia quickly reconciled. Several groups of Western oil companies, led by ExxonMobil, will soon develop Saudi Arabia's huge natural gas fields.

Saudi Arabia has all along made certain it was the largest supplier of oil to the United States; oil traders diplomats and economists said Saudi Arabia could make more money selling oil to east Asia, but has preferred to sell oil to the United States at lower prices in order to retain its coveted role.

Over the decades, the Saudis' pursuit of American money and military protection melded perfectly with America's ever-growing oil appetite to turn the two nations into reflexive allies. Saudi Arabia and the United States worked together for years to shape the balance of power in the Middle East and Central Asia.

From 1980 to 1988, the United States and Saudi Arabia armed Saddam Hussein in his war against Iran. In 1979, after the Soviet Union invaded Afghanistan, the Saudis were part of an alliance formed by the United States to drive them out.

"We collaborated in the war in Afghanistan; the Saudis, the U.S. and Pakistan," said Gregory Gause, director of Middle Eastern studies at the University of Vermont. "The Saudis had the money, the Pakistanis had the bases and we had the political oomph to get it together."

Because its interests were so densely intertwined with Saudi Arabia, the United States turned a blind eye to its ally's unsavory foreign liaisons and brewing domestic trouble.

The United States looked the other way, for instance, as the Saudi government and individuals sent money to the Taliban. Starting in 1999 and extending at least into mid-2000, Saudi Arabia exported 150,000 barrels of oil a day, gratis, to Pakistan and Afghanistan as foreign aid, according to *Petroleum Intelligence Weekly*, a trade publication. Among oil traders, it is widely believed that the shipments exceeded war-ravaged Afghanistan's needs, and that oil may have been resold to arm the Taliban.

Saudi Arabia's aid to the Taliban points up the balancing act the ruling al-Saud family has to perform between its foreign and domestic interests. The Saudis consider themselves allies of the United States. But the glue that holds their kingdom together is a puritanical strain of Islam called Wahhabism. By supporting the Taliban and other Muslim groups, the al-Saud dynasty is able to retain the goodwill of the country's clerics. Already, in response to the tacit Saudi backing of the American antiterrorism campaign, a powerful mainstream mullah in Saudi Arabia has issued a fatwa excommunicating the royal family. Fearful of protests, the Saudis have not tried to arrest him.

In fact, fear of losing power has led the Saudis to pay off just about everyone, which makes oil revenues so crucial. There is the welfare state to coddle the citizenry; the toleration of extremist clerics so that they do not stir up the masses; and the payoffs to other regimes, including a Pakistan with nuclear capability, to keep them friendly.

But that protection money has not stemmed a growing domestic restiveness, as many Saudis have become fed up with a sprawling ruling family they believe is insatiably corrupt.

"For many of the princes," said one former cabinet secretary in Washington, "the advantages of getting money exceed the advantages of keeping internal unrest down."

Many people in Saudi Arabia and the Middle East loathe the United States because they see it as the protector of a degraded regime in Riyadh. This has put pressure on the Bush administration, intent upon preserving the stability of its largest oil supplier and the appearance of Middle Eastern approval for its fight against terrorism, to toughen its stance on Israel. Prior to the assassination of an Israeli cabinet minister, some kind of shift had been expected by many, including the Israelis.

"To a certain extent," said Philip K. Verleger, an independent economist and a senior adviser in the Carter administration, "we let U.S. foreign policy be dictated to us by the house of Saud."

It is unclear what the United States can do to loosen its ties to the Saudi regime, so long as it remains reliant on its oil. Mr. Bush urged the Senate last week to get to work on a comprehensive energy policy. But the White House and most Republicans want to focus on developing domestic oil supplies. Given the fact that the United States has only 3 percent of the world's known reserves, increased drilling will do little in the long run to decrease dependence on the Middle East.

"Sept. 11 should be an alarm bell that we need a balanced, comprehensive energy policy that addresses things we don't like to do: mandating more fuel-efficient vehicles, more domestic oil and gas drilling, becoming more energy efficient as a nation," said Bill Richardson, energy secretary under President Bill Clinton.

That, in turn, could give Washington a bit more leeway in its relations with Saudi Arabia, freeing it to press for a reduction in official corruption or for reining in radical Islamic groups.

Some people, like Dan W. Reicher, former assistant secretary of energy under Mr. Clinton, think that changes that reduce American dependence on petroleum are possible without Americans having to sacrifice the kinds of cars they drive or how they live.

The question now, Mr. Reicher said, is whether Washington can find the political will to act before an oil crisis explodes.

"Will patriotism mean more than raising the flag?" he said. "Will it mean raising fuel economy?"

35

ERIC C. EVARTS

That '70s Auto Show

January 11, 2005

The ghosts of the 1973–1974 oil crisis reappeared in 2004 and 2005, when oil prices climbed steeply and to heights that had not been seen since the 1970s. With the ongoing American occupation of Iraq, along with numerous predictions of a rapidly declining supply of oil worldwide, ever higher prices at the pump, and the potential for violent clashes over the remaining oil reserves, the nonchalance about automobile fuel economy that marked the 1990s disappeared. As the following excerpt from the Christian Science Monitor *indicates, fears of future oil shocks drove car manufacturers back to the drawing board and sent consumers in search of new alternative technologies such as the hybrid vehicle.*

In an era of rising gas prices and, perhaps more particularly, war in the Middle East, words not heard in decades are peppering Detroit. Words like "efficiency" and "responsibility."

Automakers from across the globe are bragging about fuel economy, rolling out a raft of new gas-electric hybrid vehicles, and touting future autos that run on hydrogen, diesel fuel—even soybeans.

To be sure, carmakers are also buzzing about horsepower numbers and zero-to-60 times. But amid the usual flash and dash that is the annual North American International Auto Show in Detroit, the mood is unusually serious.

Eight years after Toyota launched the first hybrid car in Japan, it's traditional Detroit automakers who are trumpeting their hybrid plans and technology in nearly every presentation.

"The auto industry has a responsibility to improve emissions and fuel consumption of its cars," Rick Wagoner, CEO of General Motors Corp., told a gathering here. "We want to take the automobile out of the environmental equation. This will revolutionize the industry."

Eric C. Evarts, "That '70s Auto Show: Fuel Economy Is Back," *Christian Science Monitor*, January 11, 2005, http://www.csmonitor.com/2005/0111/p03s01-ussc.html.

The trend, driven by high oil prices, environmental concerns, and improving car technology, doesn't mean everyone will soon buy a hybrid car. But consumer taste does appear to be shifting. . . .

One result: The industry is starting to roll out hybrid versions of mainstream cars such as Honda's Civic and Accord, as well as the Ford Escape SUV.

"What's important to [hybrid buyers] is fuel economy and being politically correct, socially responsible," says Ron Pinelli, an industry analyst at Auto Data in Woodcliff Lake, N.J. Hybrids are here to stay, he says, though if fuel prices stay flat the growth of hybrids will moderate.

Hybrids reduce fuel consumption and pollution by about 30 percent compared with ordinary gasoline cars—and more than that if they use diesel power.

Hybrid sales are expected to double this year with the introduction of six new models—the Ford Escape, Toyota Highlander, Lexus 400h, Honda Accord, Mazda Tribute, and Mercury Mariner—during the 2005 model year from last September to next, says Anthony Pratt, director of analysis for advanced powertrain systems at J.D. Power Associates in Troy, Mich.

He expects hybrid sales to grow from 80,000 in 2004 to more than 400,000 by 2008.

But it remains to be seen whether Americans will continue to be willing to pay the price premium—roughly $3,000 per car—for hybrid technology long term.

Hybrid buyers tend to be the best educated and among the wealthiest buyers of any vehicle category: 40 percent have master's degrees. And 40 percent live in California. Car-buyers in middle America seldom buy hybrids, says Mr. Pratt. In part, that's because carmakers haven't marketed as much there. It's also largely because urban coastal communities provide the most conducive atmosphere for hybrids, often with higher gas prices, worse traffic, and wealthier buyers.

And the hybrids are no longer just about efficiency. They're moving upscale. Honda's new Accord hybrid, on sale since December, is the most expensive, and fastest Accord sold, in addition to the most fuel efficient. Lexus's new hybrid SUV, the 400h, is likely to cost nearly $50,000 when it rolls into dealerships this spring.

For all the questions about how fast the market will grow, one thing that seems certain is the automakers' commitment to build them.

"My grandfather's goal was to put America on wheels. My goal is to make this company a leader socially, environmentally, and economically," says Bill Ford, CEO of Ford Motor Co., preparing to introduce a range of futuristic concept cars here that included hybrids and fuel-efficient clean diesels.

36

GEORGE W. BUSH

Discussion of Hurricane Effects on Energy Supply

September 26, 2005

Since the oil crisis of 1973–1974, American presidents have felt varying pressures to develop energy policies that both meet with public approval and reflect the administration's political beliefs. In contrast to his predecessors, Ronald Reagan believed that market forces would take care of the high price of oil and bring supplies in line with demand, as is evident in Document 29. Bill Clinton had the good fortune to preside during a period of low oil prices and relatively little public pressure to formulate an energy policy. In this area, his administration will likely be remembered for the outspoken stance that his vice president, Al Gore, took regarding the United States' responsibility to lessen its greenhouse gas emissions. George W. Bush, who was in the Texas oil business during the 1970s, entered the White House in January 2001 with the hope of convincing Congress to open up the Arctic National Wildlife Refuge to drilling. Following the 9/11 terrorist attacks, his decision to invade Iraq in the spring of 2003, and the high oil prices that marked his second term in office, his administration had to address energy concerns much more substantively than anyone in the administration would have imagined before his first term. In the late summer and early fall of 2005, Hurricanes Katrina and Rita blasted the Gulf Coast and disrupted a sizable portion of the U.S. oil and gas supply. In September 2005, Bush discussed the effects of the hurricanes on the U.S. energy supply. Although he had previously emphasized the necessity of increasing the domestic production of oil and refining of gasoline, at this press conference, excerpted here, he also highlighted the need for conservation.

George W. Bush, "President Discusses Hurricane Effects on Energy Supply," September 26, 2005, http://www.whitehouse.gov/news/releases/2005/09/20050926.html.

We've just had a full briefing on what we know thus far about the effects of Hurricane Rita on the energy situation in the Gulf of Mexico.

A lot of our production comes from the Gulf, and when you have a Hurricane Katrina followed by a Hurricane Rita, it's natural, unfortunately, that it's going to affect supply. There's about 1.56 million barrels of oil that is shut in. And before Rita, just to put that in perspective, that was approximately 880,000 barrels a day that were shut in due to Katrina. So that when you really look on a map you have, if you follow the path of Katrina and the path of Rita, it pretty much covers a lot of production in the Gulf of Mexico. . . .

. . . Gasoline prices, obviously, are on our mind, and so we've watched very carefully the assessments done on the refining—the refineries there on the Gulf Coast. There are a lot of—a lot of gasoline refineries in the Houston area, in the Beaumont area, in the Port Arthur area, as well as Lake Charles, and the Louisiana area. There was about 5.4 million barrels per day that were shut in as a result of Rita and Katrina. A million of it is back up already, and we expect another 1.8 million barrels a day to get back on line relatively quickly because the storm missed a lot of refining capacity down the Texas coast. . . .

. . . We can all pitch in by using—by being better conservers of energy. I mean, people just need to recognize that the storms have caused disruption and that if they're able to maybe not drive when they—on a trip that's not essential, that would helpful. The federal government can help, and I've directed the federal agencies nationwide—and here's some ways we can help. We can curtail nonessential travel. If it makes sense for the citizen out there to curtail nonessential travel, it darn sure makes sense for federal employees. We can encourage employees to carpool or use mass transit. And we can shift peak electricity use to off-peak hours. There's ways for the federal government to lead when it comes to conservation.

And, finally, these storms show that we need additional capacity in—we need additional refining capacity, for example, to be able to meet the needs of the American people. The storms have shown how fragile the balance is between supply and demand in America. I've often said one of the worst problems we have is that we're dependent on foreign sources of crude oil, and we are. But it's clear, as well, that we're also really dependent on the capacity of our country to refine product, and we need more refining capacity. And I look forward to working with Congress, as we analyze the energy situation, to expedite the capacity of our refiners to expand and/or build new refineries.

It is clear that when you're dependent upon natural gas and/or hydrocarbons to fuel your economy and that supply gets disrupted, we need alternative sources of energy. And that's why I believe so strongly in nuclear power. And so we've got a chance, once again, to assess where we are as a country when it comes to energy and do something about it. And I look forward to working with Congress to do just that.

37

JOHN SHERFFIUS

"The Other Storm Surge"

August 30, 2005

Editorial cartoonist John Sherffius used a familiar figure from the cartoons of the 1973–1974 oil crisis, Uncle Sam, to express the fear of many Americans: that the hurricanes of 2005 would swamp consumers in a sea of rising oil prices. But as the oil crisis of 1973–1974 showed to many Americans, the nation's petroleum-based economy had other kinds of costs as well.

The other storm surge

John Sherffius, "The Other Storm Surge," August 30, 2005. John Sherffius/self-syndicated.

A Chronology of Events Related
to the Oil Crisis of 1973–1974

1859 Oil is first drilled in Titusville, Pennsylvania.

1893 The first productive oil fields are developed in California.

1901 William Knox D'Arcy receives the oil concession from Persia (later Iran). An oil well is drilled near Beaumont, Texas. The state will become a center of world oil production.

1907 Shell and Royal Dutch join to become Royal Dutch/Shell.

1910 The oil boom in Mexico begins.

1911 John D. Rockefeller's Standard Oil Company is found guilty of antitrust violations and forced to break up into separate companies.

1914 The British government acquires a 51 percent interest in the Anglo-Persian (later Iranian) Oil Company.

World War I begins and lasts until 1918. It is the first large-scale war fought with oil as a source of fuel.

1922 The oil boom in Venezuela begins.

1930 Wildcatter Columbus Marion "Dad" Joiner drills the well that will open up the East Texas oil fields.

1932 The Texas legislature gives the Texas Railroad Commission statutory authority to regulate oil production.

1933 Standard Oil of California gains a sixty-year oil concession in Saudi Arabia.

1938 Oil is discovered in Kuwait and Saudi Arabia.

The Mexican government nationalizes all foreign oil properties.

1939 World War II begins with Germany's invasion of Poland.

1941 The United States enters the war after the Japanese attack Pearl Harbor.

1943   Venezuela acquires the first "fifty-fifty" deal, whereby the government will receive about the same amount in oil royalties and taxes as the oil companies will earn in profits.

1945   World War II ends.

1947   The first residents move into the Long Island suburb of Levittown.

1948   Standard Oil of California (Chevron) and the Texas Company (Texaco) join with Standard Oil of New Jersey (Exxon) and Socony-Vacuum (Mobil) to become Aramco in Saudi Arabia.

1950   Aramco agrees to a fifty-fifty deal with Saudi Arabia.

1951   Mohammed Mossadegh becomes prime minister of Iran and nationalizes the oil industry.

1953   A coup backed by the United States and Great Britain in Iran removes Mossadegh from power.

1956   Congress passes the Federal Aid Highway Act.

Egypt's Gamal Abdel Nasser nationalizes the Suez Canal.

1959   President Eisenhower signs the Mandatory Oil Import Quota program.

1960   OPEC is established.

Congress passes the first Clean Water Act.

1962   Rachel Carson publishes *Silent Spring*.

1963   Congress passes the first Clean Air Act.

1965   President Johnson commits ground troops to the Vietnam War.

1967   Israel gains territory in the Six-Day War with Egypt and Syria.

1968   Oil is discovered on Alaska's North Slope.

Richard Nixon is elected president.

1969   The Santa Barbara oil spill occurs.

1970   President Nixon signs the National Environmental Policy Act.

Congress passes the second Clean Air Act.

Americans mark the country's first Earth Day.

1972   *Limits to Growth* is published.

Congress passes the second Clean Water Act.

Nixon is elected to a second term.

The *Washington Post* begins to publish revelations about the Watergate break-in.

OPEC presses the oil companies for a "participation" deal—that is, a greater share of the ownership of oil operations.

1973 *January*: The Paris Peace Accords end U.S. engagement in the Vietnam War.

April: James Akins publishes "The Oil Crisis."

Nixon abolishes import quotas.

Nixon forces the resignation of close aides as the Watergate scandal grows.

May: Libya shuts down its oil facilities for twenty-four hours and demands 100 percent participation.

October: Egypt and Syria attack Israel to gain back the territory lost in the Six-Day War. This is the beginning of the Yom Kippur War.

Retaliating against U.S. support for Israel, the Arab members of OPEC institute an oil embargo against the United States and the Netherlands.

OPEC begins a series of price hikes.

Vice President Spiro Agnew resigns after being charged with tax fraud. Nixon chooses House minority leader Gerald Ford to replace him.

December: Oil prices reach $11.65 a barrel, up from $2.90 a barrel before the embargo.

1974 *January*: The U.S. government discusses possible gas rationing.

March: OPEC ends the oil embargo.

August: Nixon resigns; Ford becomes president.

1975 Congress passes the Energy Policy and Conservation Act, which includes standards for automobile fuel efficiency, conservation measures, and establishment of the Strategic Petroleum Reserve.

Saudi Arabia, Kuwait, and Venezuela nationalize foreign oil operations.

North Sea oil comes online.

1977 Oil from Alaska's North Slope arrives on the market.

President Jimmy Carter delivers a nationwide address on the energy crisis.

The Department of Energy is established.

1979 Americans are taken hostage at the U.S. embassy in Iran; fifty-two are held for more than a year.

1980 Carter announces the Carter Doctrine.

The Iran-Iraq War begins.

During his presidential election campaign, Ronald Reagan calls for the Department of Energy to be abolished.

1983   Reagan approves the establishment of the United States Central Command (CENTCOM).

1986   Oil prices fall, leading to the development of larger vehicles.

1989   The *Exxon Valdez* supertanker runs aground in Prince William Sound, Alaska, spilling 11 million gallons of oil.

Protests across Eastern Europe bring down communism.

1990   Iraq's Saddam Hussein invades Kuwait.

1991   Congress approves the use of military force to liberate Kuwait, resulting in the Persian Gulf War. Retreating Iraqi troops set fire to hundreds of Kuwaiti oil fields.

The Soviet Union collapses.

2000   The economy enters a downturn.

2001   Al Qaeda attacks the World Trade Center in New York and the Pentagon in Washington, D.C.

The United States retaliates with the invasion of Afghanistan and brings down the Taliban government.

2003   The United States invades Iraq, brings down the Iraqi government, and captures Saddam Hussein. The American occupation sparks a violent insurgent movement.

2004   Oil prices begin to rise steeply.

2005   Hurricanes Katrina and Rita hit the Gulf Coast, damaging oil and gas facilities and causing a rapid increase in prices.

Questions for Consideration

1. Before the Arab oil embargo and OPEC's price hike, what issues caused some observers to grow nervous about America's oil supplies?
2. What did their concerns indicate about America's economic and political development in the post–World War II period?
3. What kind of future did environmentalists imagine if the United States (and other developed nations) did not change its dependence on oil?
4. Imagine a group of environmentalists, oil company executives, and oil policy experts in conversation in April 1973. What might they have agreed on? What would have caused disagreement among them?
5. Why did the oil embargo and price hike represent such a dramatic watershed for so many Americans? Was it really a turning point?
6. How would you characterize President Richard Nixon's response to the oil crisis?
7. What precisely made the oil embargo and price increase a crisis for the Nixon administration? What defined the end of the crisis?
8. Compare the different energy proposals put forth under the Nixon, Ford, and Carter administrations. What similarities are there? Do they use the same kind of language? What makes them different?
9. Should historians identify the 1970s as a distinct historical period because of the various oil shocks during that decade? Why or why not?
10. How did the oil crisis of 1973–1974 and its aftermath generate discussions about the proper extent of government authority? Did those discussions seem to reach any conclusions?
11. Have there been any long-term legacies of the oil crisis?
12. How would you describe the current attitude of Americans toward oil consumption, especially in comparison to that during the 1973–1974 crisis?

Selected Bibliography

Although a great many books have been written about the oil industry, relatively few histories of oil exist, especially ones based on sustained research of archival sources. By far, most of the books on oil fall under the subjects of economics, political science, and policy studies. This bibliography does not provide a comprehensive list of works on the subject of oil, but it does contain those that are especially relevant to the oil crisis of 1973–1974 and the themes explored in this volume.

The most comprehensive history of the oil industry remains Daniel Yergin's Pulitzer Prize–winning book, *The Prize: The Epic Quest for Oil, Money, and Power* (New York: Simon and Schuster, 1991). Yergin's book is especially good for understanding the international power politics of oil industry magnates before the 1960s, and it has an extensive bibliography on the oil industry.

For more about the history of oil in the United States, see, for instance, Ron Chernow's *Titan: The Life of John D. Rockefeller, Sr.* (New York: Random House, 1998) to gain insight into the most notorious oil baron. For the ultimate corporate exposé, see Ida B. Tarbell's account of the Standard Oil Company, which helped lead to the 1911 decision to break up the company: *The History of the Standard Oil Company*, 2 vols. (1904; reprint, Gloucester, Mass.: Peter Smith, 1963). Roger M. Olien and Diana Davids Olien have given us detailed accounts of the domestic oil industry, particularly in Texas and before World War II. Among their works are *Oil in Texas: The Gusher Age, 1895–1945* (Austin: University of Texas Press, 2002) and *Oil and Ideology: The Cultural Creation of the American Petroleum Industry* (Chapel Hill: University of North Carolina Press, 2000). Carl Coke Rister's 1949 book, *Oil! Titan of the Southwest* (Norman: University of Oklahoma Press, 1949), focuses on the regional development of the oil industry, especially in Texas and Oklahoma. William R. Childs looks at the role of the Texas Railroad Commission in regulating the oil industry in *The Texas Railroad Commission: Understanding Regulation in America to the Mid-Twentieth Century* (College Station: Texas A&M Press, 2005). Although Texas and Oklahoma stole the limelight in the 1920s and 1930s, California led the nation in oil production before that time. Paul

Sabin's *Crude Politics: The California Oil Market, 1900–1940* (Berkeley: University of California Press, 2005) not only explores those years but also describes a complex set of relationships between oil producers, state government, and consumers.

On the subject of the international politics of oil, the following are particularly useful: Jonathan Brown, *Oil and Revolution in Mexico* (Berkeley: University of California Press, 1993); Robert Engler, *The Politics of Oil: A Study of Private Power and Democratic Directions* (New York: Macmillan, 1961); Catherine Jayne, *Oil, War, and Anglo-American Relations: American and British Reactions to Mexico's Expropriation of Foreign Oil Properties, 1937–1941* (Westport, Conn.: Greenwood Press, 2000); David S. Painter, *Oil and the American Century: The Political Economy of U.S. Foreign Oil Policy, 1941–1954* (Baltimore: Johns Hopkins University Press, 1986); Michael Stoff, *Oil, War, and American Security: The Search for a National Policy on Foreign Oil, 1941–47* (New Haven, Conn.: Yale University Press, 1980). For a general exploration of the relationship between the United States and the Middle East, see Douglas Little's *American Orientalism: The United States and the Middle East since 1945* (Chapel Hill: University of North Carolina Press, 2002). For a detailed account of the 1953 coup in Iran, see Stephen Kinzer's *All the Shah's Men* (New York: Wiley, 2003). Nathan Citino's book *From Arab Nationalism to OPEC: Eisenhower, King Saud, and the Making of U.S.-Saudi Relations* (Bloomington: Indiana University Press, 2002) examines the very important decade of the 1950s in U.S.-Saudi relations. Robert Vitalis's work has considerably widened our knowledge of the social history of the Saudi oil fields, tying that history to patterns of frontier expansion in the United States. See Vitalis's *America's Kingdom: Mythmaking on the Saudi Oil Frontier* (Stanford, Calif.: Stanford University Press, 2007).

Postwar environmentalism in the United States has garnered increasing attention among historians. Perhaps the most synthetic political history book that exists, and which covers the 1970s, is Samuel Hays's *Beauty, Health, and Permanence: Environmental Politics in the United States, 1955–1985* (New York: Cambridge University Press, 1987). See also his collection of articles, *Explorations in Environmental History* (Pittsburgh: University of Pittsburgh Press, 1998), and Hal Rothman, *The Greening of a Nation? Environmentalism in the United States since 1945* (New York: Harcourt Brace, 1998). For a fascinating account of how postwar suburbanization contributed to the making of the environmental movement, see Adam Rome, *The Bulldozer in the Countryside: Suburban Sprawl and the Rise of American Environmentalism* (New York: Cambridge University Press, 2001). Although no historical account of the controversy over oil development in Alaska has yet been published, a relevant book is Susan Kollin, *Nature's State: Imagining Alaska as the Last Frontier* (Chapel Hill: University of North Carolina Press, 2001).

There has been very little historical work done on the oil crisis of 1973–1974, although that situation will likely change. To contextualize the events in this period, Bruce J. Schulman's *The Seventies: The Great Shift in American Culture, Society, and Politics* (New York: Free Press, 2001) is a good place to start. Scholarly analyses published shortly after the crisis remain useful. See Raymond Vernon's edited collection, *The Oil Crisis* (New York: W. W. Norton, 1976), and Joe Stork's *Middle East Oil and the Energy Crisis* (New York: Monthly Review Press, 1975). The slim collection edited by Gary Eppen, *Energy: The Policy Issues* (Chicago: University of Chicago Press, 1975), also contains some valuable essays. On the byzantine subject of oil economics, see Morris Adelman's books from the 1970s, especially *The World Petroleum Market* (Baltimore: Johns Hopkins University Press, 1972).

With the dawn of the twenty-first century, a spate of books appeared concerning the future of the global hydrocarbon society. Petroleum geologist Kenneth Deffeyes has played a prominent role in reviving the issue of peak production—that is, trying to identify when oil production will start to decline globally. See his two books on the subject, *Hubbert's Peak: The Impending World Oil Shortage* (Princeton, N.J.: Princeton University Press, 2001) and *Beyond Oil: The View from Hubbert's Peak* (New York: Hill and Wang, 2005). David Goodstein has written a very readable account of the issues related to peak production: *Out of Gas: The End of the Age of Oil* (New York: W. W. Norton, 2004). A number of writers and scholars have turned their attention both to analyzing how the United States came to depend so much on imported oil and to imagining what the future might hold. Most of these accounts are decidedly pessimistic about the latter. See Michael Klare, *Blood and Oil: The Dangers and Consequences of America's Growing Dependency on Imported Oil* (New York: Henry Holt, 2004), and Richard Heinberg, *The Party's Over: Oil, War, and the Fate of Industrial Societies* (Gabriola Island, B.C.: New Society Publishers, 2003). To see what technological options for escaping the petroleum age are available to Americans, readers can begin by consulting the work of the Rocky Mountain Institute, which can be found on its Web site, www.rmi.org.

Acknowledgments (continued from p. iv)

Document 2: Courtesy of Amherst College Archives and Special Collections.

Document 3: © 1969 U.S. News & World Report, L.P. Reprinted with permission.

Document 4: Courtesy of Amherst College Archives and Special Collections.

Document 5: Reprinted by permission of *Foreign Affairs* (vol. 51, no. 3, April 1973). Copyright 1973 by the Council on Foreign Relations, Inc.

Document 7: OLIPHANT © 1973, reprinted by permission of Universal Press Syndicate. All rights reserved.

Document 8: © 1973 The Economist Newspaper Ltd. All rights reserved. Reprinted with permission. Further reproduction prohibited. www.economist.com.

Document 9: © 1973 by National Review, Inc., 215 Lexington Avenue, New York, NY 10016. Reprinted by permission.

Document 10: Reprinted with the permission of Cartoonews International, Inc.

Document 11: Courtesy of Amherst College Archives and Special Collections.

Document 12: © 1973 Time Inc. Reprinted by permission.

Document 14: Reprinted by permission of Eric Zschiesche.

Document 15: A: © 1973 U.S. News & World Report, L.P. Reprinted with permission. B: © 1973 Time Inc. Reprinted by permission. C: © 1973 Time Inc. Reprinted by permission.

Document 16: Reprinted by permission of *The Berkshire Eagle*.

Document 17 (both): Copyright © 1974 by the New York Times Co. Reprinted with permission.

Document 18: Reprinted with the permission of David Perlman.

Document 19: Norman Podhoretz, "Doomsday Fears and Modern Life," *Commentary* 52 (October 1971): 4ff.

Document 20: Copyright © 1971 by the New York Times Co. Reprinted with permission.

Document 21: Copyright © 1973 by the New York Times Co. Reprinted with permission.

Document 22: TIME Magazine © 1973 Time Inc. Reprinted by permission.

Document 23: Reprinted by permission of the National Parks Conservation Association.

Document 24: AUTH © 1974, reprinted by permission of Universal Press Syndicate. All rights reserved.

Document 25: Copyright © 1975 by *Harper's Magazine*. All rights reserved. Reproduced from the March issue by special permission.

Document 26: © 1975 by the American Academy of Arts and Sciences. Reprinted with the permission of Zuhayr Mikdashi and MIT Press.

Document 30: From *The End of Nature* by William McKibben, copyright © 1989, 2006 by William McKibben. Used by permission of Random House, Inc.

Document 32: © 1999 Time Inc. All rights reserved.

Document 34: Copyright © 2001 by the New York Times Co. Reprinted with permission.

Document 35: Eric C. Evarts, for the *Christian Science Monitor*. Reprinted with permission.

Document 37: Reprinted with the permission of John Sherffius.

Index

Abu Dhabi, 63
Adelman, Morris, 65
advanced technology vehicles (ATVs), 147–48
Afghanistan, Soviet invasion of, 128–29, 150
Afghanistan war, 25, 135, 161
Agent Orange, 87
Agnew, Spiro, 160
air conditioning, 69, 74
aircraft, flight cutbacks, 67
air pollution, 96
Akins, James, 20, 53, 65, 160
  "The Oil Crisis: This Time the Wolf Is Here," 49–52
Alaska. *See also* Arctic National Wildlife Refuge
  North Slope oil development, 18–19, 24, 55–56, 145–46, 159, 160
  oil pipeline, 19, 70, 108
  Prince William Sound oil spill, 134
  Trans-Alaska Pipeline, 24
Al-Ateegy, Abdul-Rahman, 43
Algeria, 63, 89–90
Alliance of Automobile Manufacturers, 143
Al Qaeda, 149, 161
Al-Rifai, Rashid, 42
alternative energy
  government promotion of, 24
  potential of, 111
  as response to energy crisis, 52, 73
"America the Beautiful?" (Perlman), 88–93
American Council for an Energy Efficient Economy, 145
American Motors, 102–5
Anglo-Iranian Oil Company (AIOC), 11–12
Anglo-Persian Oil Company (Anglo-Iranian Oil Company), 8, 9, 158
anti-Americanism, 37–39
anticolonial political movements, 11–12
Apollo space mission, 88–89
Arab nations. *See also* Middle East; Organization of Petroleum Exporting Countries (OPEC); *specific nations*
  anti-Americanism, 37–39

control of oil resources by, 49–52
increase in oil prices by, 63
Israeli expansionism and, 20
nationalism, 13
opposition to U.S. policy by, 2, 20, 60, 61, 63
reduction of oil output by, 63, 66
U.S. assurances to, 13
"Arab Oil Barons Set the Pace, The" (Lurie), 59–60
Aramco, 150, 159
  anti-American sentiment and, 39
  creation of, 10
  "Memorandum to President Nixon," 60–62
  as monopoly, 14
  oil concessions, 10, 44–45
  OPEC formation and, 31–32
  U.S., Arab foreign policy and, 13–14
Aramco Agreement, 45
Arctic National Wildlife Refuge
  oil exploration and drilling in, 26, 41, 145–46, 155
  protection of, 144–46
Aswan Dam, 90–91
Athabascan tar sands, 65
Atomic Energy Commission, 68, 92
Auth, Tony
  editorial cartoon, 115
automobiles
  carpooling, 68, 73, 74, 84
  efficiency standards, 23, 134, 143–48
  environmental standards, 110
  federal, conservation policies, 68
  fuel efficiency, 101–5, 106–7, 109, 152
  gasoline rationing, 69
  hybrid vehicles, 153–55
  light trucks, 141
  postwar economy and, 15
  small car production, 101–5, 106–7
  speed limits, vii, 64, 68–69, 73, 74, 111
  sport-utility vehicles (SUVs), 26, 134, 140–41
aviation fuel, 10, 67

167